YAO MING
The Road to the NBA

By C.F. Xiao
Translated from the Chinese by Philip Robyn

LONG RIVER PRESS
San Francisco

Published in the United States of America by
Long River Press
3450 3rd St., #4B
San Francisco, CA 94124
www.longriverpress.com
Editor: Chris Robyn

Library of Congress Cataloging-in-Publication Data

Xiao, Chunfei, 1972-
[Yao Ming zhi lu. English]
Yao Ming : the road to the NBA / By Chunfei Xiao ; translated from the Chinese by
Philip Robyn.
p. cm.
ISBN 1-59265-002-3
1. Yao, Ming 1980—Juvenile literature. 2. Basketball
players—China—Biography—Juvenile literature. 3. National Basketball
Association—Juvenile literature. I. Title.
GV884.Y36X5313 2004
796.323'092—dc22

2003020704

Printed in China
10 9 8 7 6 5 4 3 2 1

Contents

Introduction: Fulfilling the Dream

The first time that I interviewed Yao Ming was on December 26, 2001, two days after I had been transferred to work in Shanghai. I went to the Hu Wan Gymnasium in Shanghai to watch a Shanghai Sharks match. Yao Ming made a dunk, and the spectators went wild, and somebody sitting next to me said, "Yao Ming really puts on a show!"Only later did I find out Yao Ming's grandmother had passed away on the 24th and that he had gone to her funeral on the 25th — Christmas Day — then rushed back to Shanghai that same night because of a game the following day. In order not to affect the emotions of his teammates, at the door of the dormitory he folded up his black arm band-a symbol of mourning-and hid it.

This was a small matter, but it made me feel that his huge body was covering a Yao Ming that nobody knew. Maybe it's only natural for the birth of a giant star to be accompanied by endless deification and lavish praise, or perhaps envy, vituperation, and overheated public commentary, often misleading people in understanding the true facts. In reality, during the course of interviews, I kept continually revising my understanding of Yao Ming as I found out what an interesting person he was.

Who in this world does not recognize Yao Ming? His flattop hair style and big, square face frequently beam forth from the covers of well-known American magazines. Sports Illustrated termed last year "The Year of Yao Ming", and an article in the weekly Time said: "In five years, Yao Ming's influence in the world will be greater than Tiger Woods." And the Japanese media have lamented that Yao Ming has already surpassed Nakata Hidetoshi as Asia's number one sports star.

If we were to sum up all of the praise and accolades for Yao Ming, we could compile a very thick book; similarly, if we were to gather together all of the writings that doubted or ridiculed Yao Ming, it would also constitute a book of significant size.

At his young age he has already had quite a taste of this callous world, and he cannot but assume a burden far heavier than those borne by others of the same age in dealing with those who, having some axe to grind, attack him or harm him through too much praise. What is astonishing is that he handles this with adroitness beyond his years. He has a strong ability to adjust psychologically, he is modest and calm, humorous and wise, and he gets along well with just about everyone. In his enormous body there beats a pure and happy heart.

He is uniquely gifted with the natural ability to play basketball, and he was born at the right time, but what allowed him to succeed was his diligence and wisdom. On his computer the screen saver displays a simple sentence: "KEEP WORK HARD."

As far as he is concerned, basketball is a dream that has always attracted him to struggle to fulfill it. He has always entered each of his new basketball worlds as an underdog. On the youth teams, he practiced like crazy to get on a team, not worrying about whether he could find shoes that would fit; once he made the team, he practiced like crazy to become a core player; once he became a core player, he practiced like crazy to win the Chinese Basketball Association (CBA) championship; once he won the CBA championship, he practiced like crazy to be able to make it to America and the NBA.

Many years ago, when Yao Ming was playing a computer version of a game based on The Three Kingdoms, one of China's greatest historical epics, there was one campaign that was hard to forget: he was using Liu Bei with 47,500 troops at the city of Ye, and he defeated Cao Cao's legion of 160,000 troops. Unlike a lot of other people, he didn't like the end game where, after one had accumulated a lot of power, one could easily run roughshod over everybody, attacking cities and ravaging the countryside. He liked the beginning of the game when there were only two or three cities — and that was the most challenging part of the game: when the beleaguered soldiers drew up beneath the city wall, scheming and strategizing to their full capacity — the weak vanquishing the strong.

He liked such situations, and matured rapidly amidst such challenges.

On the evening of January 5, 2003, an enormous "Number 15" jersey hung suspended in midair at the Hu Wan Sports Stadium in Shanghai. Yao Ming had become the first athlete in the history of Chinese sports to receive the honor of having his number retired.

Six years of hard-fought competition on the Shanghai Sharks basketball team, culminating in winning the Chinese Basketball Association championship, was a process which molded and re-

Yao Ming: The Road to the NBA

fined Yao Ming and resulted in his becoming a major presence today.

A month later, on February 10, 2003, the 52nd NBA All-Star Game unfolded at Philips Arena in Atlanta. For the 14th and last time, Michael Jordan took part in the All-Star game, and Yao Ming, in his rookie season, became the starting center. He made use of a beautiful "alley-oop" to score his first points in his first All-Star game. The star (and sentimental favorite) of the show was still Jordan, but Yao Ming was on the rise. A photograph on the official web site of the 52nd NBA All-Star Game showed Yao Ming and Jordan, with the white-clad Jordan and the red-clad Yao Ming above a caption reading: "In his last All-Star Game, Jordan will pass the baton to the hands of young players like Yao Ming."

Yao Ming's journey — one part is over, another just beginning.

1.   Childhood Past

The Yao Family of Zhen Ze

Yao Ming's ancestral home is the township of Zhen Ze, Wujiang County, Jiangsu Province, located near Shanghai. In telling someone's story, one often begins with childhood, because only in starting from childhood is there a story to tell. Moreover, tracing backwards to a person's ancestral home often turns out to be especially interesting.

Yao Ming's ancestors were definitely not kings, dukes, or aristocrats, high-ranking officials or men of great worth; and thus, it is extremely difficult to find clear traces of ordinary people in the long and slowly flowing river of history, even if one traces back only three or four generations. There are almost no meaningful records but only some narratives whose details do not completely correspond. Therefore, those who have developed an interest in the "yesterdays" of Yao Ming because of his "todays" often find some gaps. As Yao Ming's father, Yao Zhiyuan, laments today: "If we had only known that Yao Ming would become as famous as he is today, we would have grabbed a notebook and written a diary for him."

In tracing the Yao family history, people can dimly see, more than half a century ago, a newly married couple, enormously different in height, leaning on one another, walking on the esplanade at Sujia Lake, with hurried expressions, and beyond them a vast expanse of water and sky.

The man was Yao Xueming, and the wife, Xu Lizhen. They left their old home of Zhen Ze, with Shanghai as their destination. Like most other migrants in the history of Shanghai, they experienced hardships, and after finally setting down in Shanghai, there remained in the accents of the second generation a few traces of the family village dialect. The third generation — their grandson Yao Ming — spoke pure Shanghainese since childhood. Yao Xueming was a giant, a rare sight in those times, whose height was more than 6'6", while his wife was very delicate and petite. As Yao Ming's aunt, Yao Zhiying, remembers, Xu Lizhen was "about five feet tall." Yao Zhiying had never seen her own grandfather; she only remembers that her grandmother's height was considered "very tall" among women in those days.

Zhen Ze is situated southwest of Wujiang municipality, with Shanghai 72 miles to the east, and the picturesque city of Suzhou 30 miles to the north; Huzhou is 28 miles to the west. Since Zhen Ze is located in the southernmost portion of Jiangsu Province and adjoins Huzhou in Zhejiang Province in the west, in olden times it was called "Head of Wu and tail of Yue" (Wu and Yue were the names of two ancient kingdoms in China). Zhen Ze is a typical old village of the "rivers and lakes" region south of the Yangtze River, and throughout the village the nearby waterways serve as streets and as marketplaces, while ornate buildings with carved beams and painted rafters straddle the streets and narrow alleys. In nice weather, when one climbs the pagoda at Ci Yun (Charitable Clouds) Temple in Zhen Ze, the length and breadth of the rivers are spread out below like an undulating tapestry, as far as the eye can see. To the north lies Lake Tai, one of the largest in China: a vast watery region often obscured by mist.

Zhen Ze has a long history. In the year 741 (the 29th year of the Kai Yuan reign of the Tang Dynasty) prefectural governor Zhang Jingzun established Zhen Ze Hall, which marks the first appearance of the name Zhen Ze in historical records. As the fertile cradle of Wu culture, Zhen Ze has an abundance of historical sites, such as the legendary 'Dragon Beheading' Pool where Yu the Great tamed the floodwaters and beheaded the black dragon; Li Ze Lake where Fan Li raised fish; the 'Duck Raising Pool' where Lu Guimeng of the Tang Dynasty raised ducks; Zhang Pier where Zhang Zhihe, a high-ranking scholar of the Tang Dynasty, caught fish; and the 'Water Paradise Grotto' built by Yang Shaoyun, vice-president of the Song Dynasty Ministry of Rites. The local gazetteers record the 'Eight Scenic Sites of Zhen Ze' thusly: sunset at the Ci Yun Temple, flying pavilion and phoenix sail, ancient paradise, the evening vista from Rainbow Bridge, reflecting on ancient times at Zhang Pier, the sound of the Pu Ji bell, the Kang Zhuang villa, and Fan Li's fishing platform. Regrettably, several disastrous wars and the vicissitudes of history over the centuries have repeatedly devastated many of the beautiful scenes of ancient days.

The Ci Yun pagoda as it exists today is the only ancient pagoda within the confines of Wujiang Municipality; it has a history of more than 1,740 years. At the base of the ancient pagoda is the Yu Memorial Bridge, built in the 54th year of the Kang Xi reign of the Qing Dynasty to commemorate the taming of the floodwaters by Yu the Great, which is matched by the

"Bridge of Remembrance to Fan," built during the Ming Dynasty in remembrance of the worthy Fan Li on the western edge
of the ancient village. As the local literati have eulogized, "The
twisting waterways lead to land with two moon bridges, peaceful waves and willow-clad banks, and the sight of the leaning
pagoda."

Yao Xueming and Xu Lizhen, formerly so reluctant to leave
their old home, in their later years left the bustling metropolis
of Shanghai to return to their ancestral home, for a long sleep
beneath their old home ground.

Yao Xueming retired from the Gold Star Fountain Pen Factory in Shanghai, and during his life, he was no stranger to the
term "basketball." There are many versions of the story of this
6'6" worker and the game of basketball: one states that when the
Liberation Army made its way victoriously into Shanghai, Yao
Xueming quite literally stood head and shoulders above the wel-
coming crowd and made a strong impression on the comrades
responsible for sports among the troops; another says that Yao
Xueming was spotted by the sports committee among the ranks
of the National Day parade; and yet another has it that during
the time when Shanghai was celebrating public and private joint
ventures, the streets filled with the clamor of gongs and drums,
Yao Xueming was standing on the ground beating a drum, but
people thought he was standing on a bench.

The pity is that when Yao Xueming was "discovered," he
was long past training age, and so he basically could not play
basketball at all. As a trade union cadre in the factory, all he
could do was occasionally take part in the factory's amateur basketball games, wildly waving a giant hand to block shots. More

often than not, the smaller and more agile players would nimbly move past him and throw the ball into the basket. He bridled at everyone's laughter, stealthily exercising his hands that had been pained by basketball.

In 1999, Yao Xueming died at the age of 76 in a simple hovel on the old street in Zhen Ze.

Five years earlier, leading his old wife by the hand, he had returned to his native village to spend his old age, and even though he had spent most of his life in Shanghai, in his bones he was still infatuated by village life. Just two years after the passing Yao Xueming, Xu Lizhen also died.

That was on December 24, 2001. The very next day, her grandson Yao Ming arrived in a rush from Shanghai.

It was right in the midst of a battle in the CBA, and Yao Ming's team, the Shanghai Sharks, was attempting to shed the title of "second best," which it had carried for two years in a row.

The Sharks had sworn to topple the BaYi (August 1st Liberation Army) Rockets of Ningpo from its pedestal high atop the other teams in the CBA. Yao Ming himself had already been called "the little giant" for a number of years, and no one else in Chinese basketball could match him as center, neither in training nor in competition, and off the court there were always NBA scouts from America following him.

However, when Yao Ming's gigantic body knelt before his grandmother's ancestral tablet, he discovered how weak he was. Bowing his head to the ground and raising his face, he could not hold back the tears.

Yao Ming was burdened by too many expectations and doubts, too much glory and loneliness, too much triumph and tragedy, too much commendation and condemnation, too much flattery and gossip . . . and he was only 21.

In all of his 21 years, the person who loved him most dearly was his grandmother. She never knew how famous her grandson was, but she was inwardly dismayed because she was more and more often unable to see him. She was the kind that loved her grandson so much that if she thought her grandson should eat some particular food but he didn't want to eat it, he would find himself in a heap of trouble.

His petite grandmother quietly lay across from him, never to rise again. She used to always whip up heaps of food and drink for her grandson, and then she would strain her head to look upward and smile at her grandson, tall as a small mountain. That was the coldest day of the year. That morning, Yao Ming had been training, and that evening he had to rush back to Shanghai, for there was a game the following day.

In the gathering darkness, the large, tall arched stone bridges and the ancient pagoda rushed by outside the car window, and Zhen Ze Village, the place where his ancestors had lived and were buried, drew farther and farther away, and then gradually vanished.

He could not but concentrate his attention on and devote all his efforts to basketball, slam-dunking, blocking shots, and cheering with clenched fists, plus the never-ending pushing and shoving, bumping, and the 'thump' of falls to the floor.

From then on, the world forever had one less person sitting in front of the TV who loved him and was worried by that 'thump'.

Yao Ming looked around, the traces of his tears still wet. He had grown up and become a man.

Big Yao and Big Fang

"You shouldn't be called Yao Ming, you should be called Yao Pan Pan (Hopeful)"

"How come?"

"Ever since your grandfather Yao Xueming's generation, the Shanghai basketball world has been hoping for you Yaos to make a contribution to Shanghai basketball. It's too bad that by the time your grandfather was discovered, he was already too old and couldn't play ball; later, it was hoped that your father would play ball for Shanghai, but he was delayed by the Cultural Revolution; and now the hopes are on you. . . ."

This was a conversation that year between Yao Ming and Wang Zhongguang, a famous veteran of Shanghai basketball.

Yao Zhiyuan, Yao Ming's father, was born in 1951. He was the first child of Yao Xueming and Xu Lizhen, and in 1967, after the "going up to the mountains and down to the country-side" campaign began, Yao Zhiyuan had just graduated from junior high school. As the eldest son of the Yao family, he was naturally added to the roster of "young intelligentsia."

At that time, Yao Zhiyuan had already trained in basketball for a period at the Xu Jia Hui District Youth Sports School. He had grown to over 6'5" in height, and the Shanghai sports work teams had had their eyes on him for some time.

That year, Wang Zhongguang and others who were then playing in Shanghai men's basketball got hold of the military administration cadre:

"Is there some way to keep Yao Zhiyuan from being sent down to the countryside?"

"Oh, we can't do that!"

"But just look at him, sir! Yao Zhiyuan is over 6'5"." It just wouldn't be fitting for him to be carrying a shoulder pole in some farm village. Please see if you can take care of it. . . ."

With every possible persuasion having been tried, Yao Zhiyuan wasn't sent to the countryside but stayed on as a worker at a factory in Xu Jia Hui.

The unexpected good luck was that, beginning in 1968, the "campaign of going up to the mountains and down to the countryside" started to emphasize "Red through and through," and everybody had to go to the vastness of the rural villages to receive disciplinary training. That year, Yao Zhiyuan's younger sister, Yao Zhiying, graduated from junior high school and had no choice but to go to the countryside. Because of her father and elder brother, Yao Zhiying had also trained in basketball at the youth sports school for a period of time during that year. Her coach felt that she might also grow to be very tall, so she got to train for half a year, but Yao Zhiying's height of 5'3" seemingly did not change in the least, so the coach finally gave up, and even though Yao Zhiying really loved basketball, she had to put down the ball and return home, and then she went to the countryside — to her mother's old home, Qin Xing Village on the outskirts of Zhen Ze. She later married there and had a child, and did not move back to Shanghai.

Although Yao Zhiyuan remained in the city, he was not

1. Yao Ming's hometown: Zhen Ze, Wujiang County, Jiangsu Province. (Author photo).

2. Another view of Zhen Ze (Author photo).

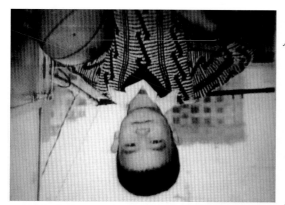

4. Yao Ming (far right) with friends in 1983 (Author photo).

5. With his mother at the Great Wall (Author photo).

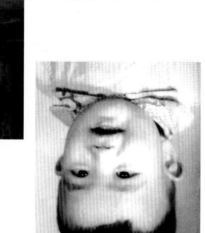

6. The Young Hoopster (Author photo).

3. As a youngster (Author photo).

7. With childhood friend Wang Jiayin, 1988 (Author photo).

8. With Wang Jiayin in 1993 (Author photo).

9. Training with the Shanghai youth team (Author photo).

12. *Playing against the Ba Yi Rockets*
(Fan Jun / Xinhua).

11. *In August 2001, Yao Ming injured his*
ankle in a match against Yugoslavia while
playing on the Chinese national team.
(Li Jundong / Xinhua).

10. *Training is hard!*
(Author photo).

13. *As a member of the Shanghai Sharks team in the Chinese Basketball Association (Author photo).*

14. Yao Ming was voted most valuable player of the 2000-2001 Chinese Basketball Association season (Li Yue / Xinhua).

15. Participating in a charity junction with tennis star Andre Agassi during the Shanghai Open tennis tournament, September 2001 (Fan Jun / Xinhua)

16. Shooting against the Jiangsu Dragons team, November 2001. The Sharks defeated the Dragons to enter the playoffs (Liu Dawei / Xinhua).

17. Going for the ball with Wang Zhizhi of the BaYi Rockets, November 2001 (Zhuang Jin / Xinhua).

18. On April 19, 2002 the Shanghai Sharks win the 2001-2002 CBA championship. Yao Ming hoists the trophy (Wang Xiaochuan / Xinhua).

19. During the World Championships, the Chinese team lost to the U.S. 65 to 84, but Yao Ming made a big impression (Wang Yan / Xinhua).

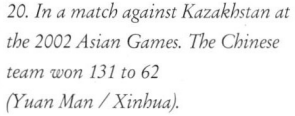

20. In a match against Kazakhstan at the 2002 Asian Games. The Chinese team won 131 to 62 (Yuan Man / Xinhua).

allowed to play basketball. Wang Zhongguang and the others again sought out the military administration cadre, with the idea of having Yao Zhiyuan transferred into a sports work team, but they were flatly denied: "No! Do you want me to commit a political error?"

This situation dragged on until 1970 before Yao Zhiyuan finally joined a sports work team. Even today, Wang Zhongguang is still filled with regret: "He already missed the best opportunity for systematic training." Afterwards, Yao Zhiyuan became the starting center for the Shanghai team, and was chosen for the national collective training team, but he was never able to become a member of the national team. He originally should have been able to advance higher in his sports career, but political movements obliterated his talent.

In 1979, Yao Zhiyuan retired from military service and was dispatched to a position as a worker in the Shanghai Bureau of Maritime Affairs. Eighteen years later, his son, Yao Ming, also joined the Shanghai men's basketball team. Both father and son wore number 15.

By contrast, Yao Ming's mother, Fang Fengdi, had a more illustrious career than her husband; she was formerly the captain of the Chinese women's basketball team. Fang Fengdi was Shanghainese. In 1966, as the first waves of the Chinese Cultural Revolution swept throughout China, she had already joined the Shanghai women's basketball team and begun to lead the relatively cloistered life of an athlete at the age of 14.

Fang Fengdi was, without a doubt, more fortunate than Yao Zhiyuan, as she did not miss the optimal age for receiving systematic training.

From September 1 through 16 of 1974, the Seventh Asian Games were held in Tehran, Iran. These were the first Asian Games to which China sent teams following the restoration of China's legal membership in Asian sports organizations. China won 33 gold medals and was ranked third in terms of total gold medals won. Fang Fengdi was captain of the Chinese women's basketball team and took part in the women's basketball competition: it was the first time that a Chinese women's basketball team participated in the Asian Games.

At that time, the coaches of the Chinese basketball team were Cheng Shichun, Qian Chenghai, and Hu Lide, and members of the women's basketball team included Fang Fengdi, Yang Shuying, Wang She, Zhu Qihui, Wang Naifeng, Wang Yuzhen, Wei Wenshan, Li Muzhen, Du Huanwen, Liu Yumin, Chen Xiushan, and Luo Xuelian.

The Chinese women's basketball team ended up winning the bronze medal.

Subsequently, on November 2 through 12, 1976, the Sixth Asian Women's basketball Championship was held in Hong Kong, and this was the first time that a Chinese women's basketball team participated in the Asian Women's Basketball Championship after restoration of China's legal membership in the Asian Basketball Federation. On November 12, the Chinese women's basketball team defeated the South Korean team by a score of 73 to 68. The South Korean team had previously won the Asian women's basketball championship four times.

At the start of the final match, the Chinese team made a lot of mistakes, and the South Korean team went on a run, scoring again and again; the Chinese team was trailing 10 to 2. The Chinese team collected themselves and faced the challenge, strengthened their defense, and managed to catch up, 23 to 24. The South Korean team sank several perimeter shots, widening the score again. At the end of the first half, the Chinese team trailed 31 to 43.

In the second half, the Chinese team made some adjustments to their lineup, enlarged their defensive zones, solidified their inside defense, strengthened their rebounding, put together some fast breaks, and played double centers with Fang Feng Di and Song Xiaobo trading places. Coordinating the inside and outside, and working together with tacit understanding, they penetrated their opponent's tight defense, repeatedly winning the battle under the basket, confounding their opponent's formations, and gradually narrowing the score. With only six minutes left in the second half, Song Xiaobo got free under the basket and went up to score, making the score 63 to 62 and putting the Chinese team in the lead for the first time. Following this, the Chinese team grew braver and braver, leading the rest of the way and winning the game.

Fang Fengdi still remembers the joy of final victory after that fierce competition — the awards ceremony was held immediately after the game, and when the emotionally charged Chinese team filed onto the court, more than a thousand spectators responded with long and enthusiastic applause and cheers.

In that era when sports bore the heavy burden of politics, Fang Fengdi received a not insignificant "political remuneration" for her outstanding achievements. On September 30, 1974, Premier Zhou Enlai hosted a grand reception at the Great Hall of the People in Beijing to ardently celebrate the 25th anniversary of the founding of the People's Republic of China, and Fang

Fengdi attended as the sports representative. On the evening of August 1, 1977, the Ministry of Defense held a grand reception at the Great Hall of the People to celebrate the 50th anniversary of the founding of the Chinese People's Liberation Army, and Fang Fengdi also attended as the sports representative.

But in the end, fame and glory abated into silence, and Fang Fengdi retired at about the same time as Yao Zhiyuan. Because of her special achievements, she received an assignment befitting her specialty, entering the Shanghai Sports Science Institute.

Yao Zhiyuan was 6'8" tall, and Fang Feng Di was 6'1". Not surprisingly, their close acquaintances were accustomed to calling them 'Big Yao' and 'Big Fang'. When they were married, they were dubbed "the first married couple of Asia."

This husband and wife, who had struggled so hard and made such sacrifices for the cause of Chinese basketball, now began a prosaic life, and were gradually forgotten by the fans who had once cheered for them.

But their contributions to Chinese basketball did not end with their retirement; on the contrary, their greatest and most exciting contribution was about to begin.

On September 12, 1980, their son Yao Ming was born.

A Time of Simple Joy

Perhaps when he grows old, Yao Ming will return in his

dreams to Number 95 Kang Ping Road in Shanghai, amidst the clamor of his childhood friends.

The plain and happy childhood of Yao Ming's memory unfolded in a corridor that today seems narrow and short. This corridor is a testament to the housing shortage experienced in Shanghai in the 1980s: in a simple six-story building, each floor held six households, the layout being "a room and a half," which is one room of approximately 40 square feet, with southern exposure plus another small living room or bed room of 20 square feet, with the units on each floor all using the same corridor. Room 602 was somewhat different from its neighbors: at that time, each of the doors had a "vent window," but the "doors" inside Room 602 had no door frames, being joined together with the "vent windows" in one piece. As Yao Zhiyuan, the owner of this unit, was too tall, and had the doors had frames, he would have bumped his head if he wasn't careful.

The residents of this building were all staff of the Shanghai Municipal Sports Committee. At that time, the Shanghai Municipal Sports Committee, in order to alleviate the housing shortage for its staff, built a simple building on this spot, behind which was a track and field stadium, and people used to call it "the wind and rain sports field." Later, a "championship building" was also constructed here, wherein resided the famous Zhu Jianhua, who had broken the world high-jump record three times.

Wang Liangzuo, current head coach of the Chinese women's tennis team, Shen Fulin, head coach of the Shanghai men's volleyball team, and others all lived close to the Yao family at that time. The rooms were small, and the corridor became the children's playground.

"I never imagined that someone who was so stiff and ill at

ease when he was little would now have become a worldwide basketball star!" said Zhang Fang of Yao Ming, but with a sisterly tone; in fact Yao Ming had called her "Big Sister Fang-Fang" for twenty years.

Yao Ming grew up with Zhang Fang, Wang Jiayin, Sun Yi, and Sun Jiachuan. Zhang Fang was the oldest and the most mischievous, like a boy, and sometimes she would "freak out" and raise such hell that the adults had to "separate" her with an iron gate, but she still would not calm down, and she would play cards with Wang Jiayin through the iron gate. Yao Ming was second oldest of the five children, but Yao Ming was easy-going and compliant with a temperament almost like a girl. When they played cops and robbers, Yao Ming always took the role that no-one wanted. When they all played card games together, Yao Ming had the most paper strips stuck on his face, because the others would gang up on him. Yao Ming knew this, but it didn't bother him; his face would be covered with a simpering smile.

Everybody loved to watch Yao Ming play hide and seek. Everyone would look for a place to hide, and Yao Ming would turn this way and that, left and right, craning his head first in one direction and then in another, but he was never able to find anybody. At the end of his rope, Yao Ming would have to ask Zhang Fang's father for help: "Zhang Fang's daddy, where are they?"

Zhang Fang's father liked to tease Yao Ming, so he would point in a random direction and say, "Over there, over there!"

Yao Ming, hearing a sound, would go over and turn every corner inside out; confused and disoriented, he still was not able to find anybody. Every time this happened, but every time he still liked to play together with the gang.

Sometimes he would be hit by Zhang Fang, but he wouldn't hit back, nor would he argue; rather, he would go to find Zhang Fang's father: "Zhang Fang's daddy, Zhang Fang hit me."

"If she hits you once, hit her back twice."

"Oh, no! My mama says you aren't supposed to hit people."

Zhang Fang later summed it up: "Yao Ming only knew how to be a tattletale, he never fought back."

Even today, Zhang Fang still likes to knock on Yao Ming's big head, but she has to wait until he sits down before she can reach it.

Fang Fengdi remembers that "As a person, Yao Ming was straightforward and honest, and he never caused us any trouble." But just like all the children, Yao Ming got spanked. There was one time when a neighbor kid came to the Fangs' house with a complaint, saying that Yao Ming had picked on him. Fang Fengdi and Yao Zhiyuan thought about it — Yao Ming was so tall, he *must* have picked on the other boy. So when Yao Ming got home, his parents mercilessly criticized him, finally saying, "Go apologize to him!"

Yao Ming made not a sound while receiving this scolding. Then, when Fang Fengdi learned more of the details, she found that it had been the other child who had picked on Yao Ming, that the "villain" had told on him first. Subsequently, whenever this type of incident happened, his parents would ask questions and get to the bottom of things. "It can be said responsibly that, even though he is so big, Yao Ming has never bullied anyone."

A great many people who came into contact with Yao Ming said to Fang Fengdi, "Your child is too simple and honest, and he'll suffer for it when he grows up."

Fang Fengdi says, "I believe that if Yao Ming treats others with honesty, others will also treat him with honesty."

When he was two or three years old, Yao Ming didn't appear taller than his little gang of playmates; in fact, he seemed somewhat pudgy — you have to know that when he was born at the Shanghai Sixth People's Hospital he weighed close to 11 lbs., and caused his mother Fang Fengdi considerable suffering. Afterwards, he grew taller and taller, causing Wang Jiayin to complain that "we only see Yao Ming growing, but we don't see us growing." Wang Jiayin is the national collegiate tennis champion, and only 5'7" compared to Yao Ming.

There was one spring when the five children all went on a bike trip to the suburbs together, and on the way they encountered several power poles that were leaning way over. A normal person would have been able to get past easily, but Zhang Fang, who was riding in the lead, suddenly thought of Yao Ming behind, and hurriedly turned her head around to yell, "Yao Ming, be careful, hurry up and duck your head!"

Zhang Fang has always been moved by a small event: when she was attending the third year of middle school, Yao Ming's family had earlier moved away from Kang Ping Road, but she still lived in the same place. One weekend, a home tutor was teaching Zhang Fang remedial lessons when Yao Ming suddenly appeared before her, which gave her quite a start. "Elder Sister Fang Fang, today I just happened to be passing by your building, so I thought I would come up to see you," Yao Ming said. Zhang

Fang was just in the middle of her lesson, and although they had not seen one another for a long time, the two parted after exchanging only a few words. Even today, Zhang Fang finds it hard to forget her feelings at that moment.

"A good child who understood proper behavior, never rushed in without knocking, and never raised a ruckus." This was the "summation" of Jin Qingxiang, Wang Jiayin's maternal grandfather, with regard to Yao Ming. In those years when Jin went to Kang Ping Road to visit his granddaughter, Yao Ming would always be standing by the door and would always address him, "Grandpa," and then stay by the door without moving. Jin Qingxiang would beckon to him, "Come in, hurry and come in." Only then would Yao Ming slowly amble in.

Wang Jiayin still keeps a tape recording containing the refined singing voice of Yao Ming. That day, Wang Jiayin was celebrating her fourth birthday, and Yao Ming, who was a year older, offered a song to the "little birthday girl," singing a song he had learned in nursery school. After singing a few lines, he forgot the words, then continued, then forgot more of the words. Everybody held their sides laughing, and Yao Ming, his big head swaying to the rhythm, kept on singing.

There was one time when Yao Ming came through Wang Jiayin's front door and Wang Jumei, Wang Jiayin's maternal grandmother, got something for him to eat.

Yao Ming very politely refused: "I won't have anything to eat."

"This is from grandma — you have to eat it."

Yao Ming turned around and retreated: "I'll go ask Mama."

Today, whenever the subject of Yao Ming is raised, Wang Jumei continues to praise him to no end: "Big Fang and Big Yao raised him right." She says that Fang Fengdi and her husband were strict with their son ever since he was little, and this is why Yao Ming is so good-natured and never acquired any bad habits. Now that he has become famous, become a big star, he is still modest and prudent, and isn't "cocky."

When Wang Jiayin was in her first year of high school, there was one time when she went with her schoolmates to the Hu Wan Gymnasium to see Yao Ming play. Everyone was yelling and cheering for Yao Ming, and Wang Jiayin boasted, "I grew up with Yao Ming!"

Her classmates didn't believe her, and they got out their notebooks and made her go get Yao Ming's autograph. So Wang Jiayin tried to get into the athletes' lounge, but the doorman would not let her in. Wang Jiayin wrote a note: "Yao Ming, this is Wang Jiayin, I'm waiting for you at the door, but they won't let me in." The slip of paper was passed in, and right away Yao Ming came running over and autographed all five or six notebooks that Wang Jiayin had brought in one breath.

The family of Shen Jiachuan was the earliest to move away from Kang Ping Road; then Yao Ming's family moved to Shuang Feng Road, and Wang Jiayin and the others also moved away one by one. However, nobody ever forgot their annual get-together.

That day is a holiday for the five of them.

Concerns of Youth

To the sound of the Chinese national anthem, the young flag raiser slowly raised the national flag, and nobody noticed the look of envy on the face of elementary school student Yao Ming standing in the last row.

Many years later, on October 19, 2002, when Yao Ming was to leave China the following day to begin his career in the NBA, he returned to his alma mater, the Gao An Road First Elementary School in Shanghai, and revealed to his former teachers the dream of his youth: "After I started elementary school, I hoped I could be a glorious flag raiser."

"Glorious flag raiser" was the honor given to the students with the highest academic achievement by the Gao An Road First Elementary School, but Yao Ming had never been chosen, something he still regrets today.

"Yao Ming was a good student, and his academic achievement was not bad; his deportment was also good, but at the time he was timid and not able to express his desires, so the teachers didn't notice him," said Ni Jing, the teacher in charge of Yao Ming's third- and fourth-grade classes.

When Yao Ming went to third grade, he was already 5'6" tall. Of course, at that time Yao Ming's father was even taller, and each time he came to pick up Yao Ming after school he stood out from the other parents gathered outside the window looking about; Yao Zhiyuan's head rose above the vent window above the classroom door, and whenever he saw this, Ni Jing would say, "Yao Ming, your dad's here."

But what is most deeply engraved in Ni Jing's memory is not Yao Ming's height but rather this student's "thickness," that is, his honesty and sincerity: "The class had organized a spring outing to the park, and at that time conditions were not as good as now, and there weren't enough seats on the bus, so some people had to stand. Yao Ming never sat, and always gave his seat to a smaller classmate."

The Gao An Road First Elementary School, located at Kang Ping Road, Lane 4, Number 9, is one of Shanghai's well-known schools. Before Yao Ming, it had produced a number of other famous athletes such as national volleyball player Shen Fulin. But in those early years, none of the teachers thought that Yao Ming would become a basketball superstar. Ni Jing says, "He was a very dedicated student and didn't need special help with remedial lessons from the teachers. He was very disciplined, not like a lot of physically gifted students who cannot keep up academically."

Gong Lingzhen, the teacher in charge of Yao Ming's first-grade class, was only 4'10"; the first time she saw Yao Ming she was startled: "Ai Ya! This first-grader is as tall as the teacher!" When Yao Ming came to bid her farewell before going abroad, the old lady strained to look up at him, almost falling over, before she could take him all in.

But in the eyes of Gong Lingzhen, Yao Ming was still that well-behaved child sitting in the very last row. "Although he was very tall then, he was very mild and compliant, and he never used his height to bully the smaller classmates; sometimes he would even be bullied by the smaller students. Then I would tell him that if someone picks on you, you come and tell me."

In first and second grade, the teachers' office was always Yao Ming's refuge, but when he got to third and fourth grade, nobody picked on Yao Ming, for everyone discovered that Yao Ming was truly a good child and got along very well with his classmates. He didn't have too much to say, but by nature he was not unsociable, and he was always happy to help others.

Teacher Gong Lingzhen was no longer in charge of his class, so he didn't often go to Teacher Gong's class to help sweep and clean, because Teacher Gong's first- and second-grade classes still didn't do too many activities. Actually, from the time he began fourth grade, Yao Ming took complete charge of the task of cleaning all of the tall windows at the Gao An Road First Elementary School, and teachers of any of the grades would call out: "Yao Ming, come help us clean the windows." And Yao Ming never tired of doing it.

Gong Lingzhen was an elementary school teacher for 36 years, and she is now retired and stays at home. She is a product of the traditional educational environment, the kind of person who will always staunchly believe that "the teacher is the engineer of the human soul," and she firmly believes that character education is more important than educating the intellect. Even today, she still espouses "the need to properly train the nation's successors." She spent her entire life accompanying the children of the lower elementary grades, and she is poor but happy throughout and has a heart as pure and true as that of a child.

The first thing she does is to instill in the children the word "love."

"You must love your classmates, and friends must love one another; do not fight or wrangle." She would lecture in front of the blackboard, and Yao Ming, hands clasped behind his back, would sit in the last row, listening attentively.

When he first began to receive an education, Yao Ming deeply committed this sentence to memory: "If you are picked on by others, there will always be some way to reason it out." Gong Lingzhen says that from a very young age Yao Ming always cultivated a generous and magnanimous character, and never haggled with others.

At that time, in Gong Lingzhen's eyes, Yao Ming, whose height did not match his actual age, was a very well-behaved and obedient child, very dedicated to his studies. His achievement was generally "good," though not enough to be "superior." Teacher Gong humorously sums it up thusly: "Yao Ming's brain and body were growing at the same time, so how could they both manage to grow sufficiently?"

When he first started school, Yao Ming's enunciation was not too clear, and when he spoke he would lower his eyes and not look straight ahead but always at the floor, so during class Gong Lingzhen would always ask him questions: "Yao Ming, you answer this question." Or she would have him read the lesson aloud. On the one hand, she wanted to give Yao Ming opportunities to enhance his ability to express himself verbally, and on the other hand, Yao Ming sat in the last row and was easily distracted.

"I think Yao Ming's verbal skills are now quite good," laughed Gong Lingzhen. "When he is being interviewed by reporters, he looks directly at the other person and speaks very well." She feels that her speech training of Yao Ming from a young age was quite effective.

Yao Ming was better in language arts than in math. When he learned to write in first and second grade, he was the most serious student in his class. When they were copying characters, stroke by stroke, and a character didn't come out well, he would immediately erase it and write it again until it matched the example in the square grid pattern. It's too bad that he couldn't keep this habit for long, and today Yao Ming's handwriting is nothing special. In math he very seldom got a perfect score; Gong Lingzhen says, "Yao Ming tended to be a bit careless, and he usually got 90 per cent."

Yao Ming has deep feelings for Gong Lingzhen. After graduating from elementary school, he would go back to visit her on Teachers' Day every year, and when he was out of town for a game and missed Teachers' Day, he would go make it up after he returned. Later on, Gong Lingzhen was transferred to another job at the Yuan Ping Road branch of the Gao An Road First Elementary School, and she also went to the Ai Ju Primary School to serve as a teacher for a time. So Yao Ming often failed to find her on his visits, but he never stopped coming; he would ask around, for he had to find her and see her face to face, if only to say a short phrase: "Happy Teachers' Day!"

Whenever Gong Lingzhen remembers this she is very moved: "When other students made their way back to Gao An Road First Elementary School but couldn't find me, they would just give up. Yao Ming's loving heart is really something special."

When he returned to his alma mater before going abroad, Yao Ming strode directly to his former first grade classroom, for he knew the way; however, the classroom door was locked, so he shouted, "Where's my teacher?" Someone else told him that his teacher was waiting on the third floor, so he clomped up to the third floor. Gong Lingzhen, who was waiting there, smilingly accepted a bunch of flowers from her former student and then gave him another lesson: "If you're going to compete with foreigners you'll have to train to be a little stronger. When my husband and I used to watch you play, I used to worry whenever somebody knocked you down."

2. Young Hoopster

In Love With Basketball

During the 2002 world championship, the last question that an ESPN reporter asked Yao Ming was, "When your professional career is over, what would you like people to remember about Yao Ming?"

Yao Ming thought for a minute and then answered earnestly, "I don't know exactly which words to use to accurately express it, but I hope that through me they will have a greater interest in basketball, that they will know that this is a great sport worthy of involvement; this is what I would like people to remember and understand through me."

The world's first basketball game took place 112 years ago. In fact, it was on December 21, 1891, at the YMCA school gymnasium at Springfield College in Massachusetts. At that time, there was no such thing as a basketball, so what the players contested with was a soccer ball, and the player who got the ball used all sorts of strange postures to throw this soccer ball — which had no special feel to it — into a basket which the local farmers used to pack peaches.

No one thought that this sport would subsequently become popular worldwide or could make a Chinese named Yao Ming world-famous.

At that time, Dr. James Naismith, physical education instructor at the YMCA, Springfield College, Massachusetts, was looking for a way to develop sports activities during the winter, and he had thought many times about moving certain activities indoors. On various occasions he had tried football, soccer, and lacrosse, all without success. Because a football rolls so vigorously and unpredictably, it is difficult to play football indoors on a hard surface; after soccer was moved indoors, a lot of players were injured and the glass in all the windows was broken, With lacrosse, because of the limitations of the court, the students would often get all tangled together and hit each other with their sticks, turning the games into armed clashes.

By the middle of the 19th century, most of the modern Olympic sports had already been born; for example, soccer was created in 1863, and tennis in 1873. Naismith realized that if he tried to move some already-developed sport indoors it would be difficult to obtain a good result, and that he would have to adopt features of particular sports and combine them to form a new sport that the students would like. He analyzed various kinds of sports and found that for all of the sports using a smaller ball some sort of implement was used to control the ball, thus complicating the technique and making it difficult to grasp. So he decided to use a large ball that could easily be controlled by the hands.

Inspired by a peach orchard workers' and children's game of throwing for accuracy toward a "peach basket" and by a hit-the-target game called "duck on the rock" that he himself had played as a child, Dr. Naismith nailed two peach baskets to the balcony rails at each end of the gymnasium floor at a height of about 10 feet, which is approximately the same height as the modern basket, and chose a British soccer ball for throwing into the baskets; a ball thrown into the basket earned one point, the number of points determining the winner.

The first experimental game was held in the YMCA gymnasium on December 21, 1891; participants were the students of the secretarial class which Naismith taught. The class, which totaled 18 students, was divided into two teams, and the game was started by tossing the ball up between the two team captains, Frank Mahan and Duncan Peyton, and then the contest between the two sides began. Because they struggled so intensely, the students became very excited, and during the game one student named Willems R. Kase made a shot; the game ended with a score of 1 to 0.

This was the first score in the history of basketball.

Because this kind of game was fiercely competitive, very interesting, and easily grasped, the students really liked it a lot, and it soon began to gain popularity in America. After the birth of this new sport, the most pressing task was to give it a new name. Naismith's student Frank Mahan suggested to him that it be called "Naismith Ball," but Naismith adamantly disagreed. Then Mahan suggested that perhaps it might be called "basket ball," and when Naismith heard this he was in complete agreement: "We used two baskets and one ball, so the name basketball is very suitable." Thus was basketball born.

When it was first created, the game of basketball did not have any limits with regard to the number of players or court dimensions, and when the ball had been thrown into the basket, it was necessary to climb a ladder to retrieve the ball before play could continue. Later on, impatient players cut a large hole in the bottom portion of the basket webbing.

Dr. Naismith's early form of basketball underwent many years of evolution before developing into what Yao Ming referred to as "a great sport worthy of participation," and it also took Yao Ming many years before he came to like the sport.

The first time Yao Ming ever shot a basket was when he was in first grade. The Gao An Road First Elementary School was going to hold a sports meet — actually, it would be a bit more appropriate to call it a 'game gathering' — where the young students would playfully run around a circle to see who was fastest and shoot baskets to see who was the most accurate shooter.

"Students, who should we have in the basket-shooting contest?" asked the teacher in charge, Gong Lingzhen, from the rostrum, her eyes looking at Yao Ming seated in the last row. Actually, she didn't even have to hint, for all the youngsters burst out at once: "Yao Ming!"

Everyone knew that Yao Ming's father and mother were basketball players, and the fact that Yao Ming had already grown to a height of nearly five feet in the first grade gave the teacher and his classmates even more reason to pin their hopes on him.

"When my classmates yelled my name, at that instant I felt very, very . . . how should I put it, just like I felt after I took the championship later on," Yao Ming remembers.

His two hands pressed to the seams of his pants, he stood up, a dignified look on his face, and looked around proudly.

This little boy, who many years later would become the very best in the NBA, stood before a simple and crude basket and began the first shot of his life — he stood behind the foul line, his two hands gripping the ball and holding his breath, but his heart was beating wildly, and his two arms and the ball pressed tight to his chest seemed to be trembling with the beating of his heart.

However, his shot didn't go into the basket, but feebly hit the backboard, fell to the ground, bounced a few times, and rolled away off to the side.

Yao Ming was stunned, and the whole class, who had been waiting to applaud, looked at one another in disbelief. And what happened next made Yao Ming even more red-faced: another smaller classmate held the basketball with both hands, and with a very amateurish motion — a double underhand shot, or "dumping the bucket" in basketball jargon — threw the ball up and made a basket!

"I was just really so embarrassed!" Even today, Yao Ming remembers what a difficult position he was in at that time. He was someone who really wanted to exert his efforts for the honor of the class. His grades in studying were ordinary, he didn't love to talk, and he wasn't good at showing off in front of the teacher. Except for his height, he had no other qualities that would make people notice him.

Teacher Gong Lingzhen says that, although even from a young age Yao Ming never displayed any basketball talent, she would say that "he could bounce a rubber ball pretty good."

In the young students' activities class, Gong Lingzhen had the children compete at bouncing rubber balls to see who could bounce the most, and this later developed into "fancy bouncing," with the youngsters bouncing the ball behind their backs, under lifted legs, and bouncing while walking, and it was quite a boisterous activity. Yao Ming was tall and had long arms and lots of strength, so he had the advantage in these activities — however, in another ball activity, the tall Yao Ming was at a disadvantage: this activity was called "hitting the wild duck," which is basically like dodge ball: where the students formed a circle around one person in the middle, and everyone took turns throwing the rubber ball at that person to see whether he could dodge it.

After Yao Ming became a number-one center, a lot of people said that he had loved basketball ever since he was little, and that his parents had practiced playing ball with him from a young age. But Yao Ming, Yao Ming's parents, and his teachers and coaches, as well as his companions at that time, all say that at first he didn't like basketball at all, and that during those years basketball was just another game to him.

Yao Ming's father, Yao Zhiyuan, says that when Yao Ming was little he was just like other boys: first he liked guns, then he liked to read books, especially books about geography. For a time he was even interested in archaeology, and then he liked building model ships. "I remember the first time he got a paycheck from the physical education work unit, he went and bought a model ship and built it himself. And then after that, he liked game machines."

Yao Ming's cousin, Qian Yao, has boundless memories of the two of them playing with electric cars under the bed. "He was especially interested in warship models, and when he was little I never heard him say anything about wanting to play basketball."

Later on, like most Chinese urban children of the 1980s, Yao Ming liked to go out and play video games. At that time, he had not yet entered the Youth Sports School to play basketball, and during summer vacation he liked to go to his aunt's house in Zhen Ze to play. Qian Yao remembers that there was one time when he was busy and couldn't play with Yao Ming, so he urged several of his friends that his cousin, Yao Ming, was very young, and when they took him to go out to play games, they would have to take good care of him; but when Qian Yao's friends saw how big Yao Ming was, they stuck out their tongues and said, "Maybe he'd better take care of us."

When he was nine years old, Yao Ming went to the Xu Jia Hui District Youth Sports School to train in basketball. Sometimes when he felt like it, Yao Zhiyuan would play basketball with Yao Ming beside the old carport in front of the dormitory — Yao Ming seemingly still lacked a spirit of "respect for this calling," because every time after his son made a few baskets, Yao Zhiyuan had to buy him some little toy to reward him. Later on Yao Ming said teasingly, "In the beginning, I relied on receiving bribes to play basketball."

After he had been at the Xu Jia Hui District Youth Sports School for a little longer, Yao Zhiyuan, together with alumni of the Shanghai men's basketball team like Li Qiuping, and Wang Qun would play against Yao Ming and his group of young teammates. On the court, Yao Ming had the job of guarding his dad, and he was often bested in this one-on-one match up, but after Yao Ming grew up, Yao Zhiyuan then became no match for him, and Li Qiuping and Wang Qun later became Yao Ming's coaches.

Fang Fengdi says that when Yao Ming was sent to the Youth Sports School to train in basketball during those years, although at the time he didn't really like basketball, he nevertheless went without saying another word, and he trained very hard: "He was an obedient child."

"It was probably around 1998 to 1999 that I first started to like basketball." Yao Ming remembers. "When I first started, it was kind of like I was half being forced into it, purely because at the time my parents were basketball players, and I also felt like I was doing it for their benefit, and so I said that no matter what, I would just have to do my best and stick it out. But I didn't know why I went to play basketball. So I eventually joined a basketball team; maybe it was just my fate. Then in 1998-1999 I played in a lot of international competitions, and then, especially after playing in the 2000 Olympics, I realized how marvelous high-level basketball was!"

Because he was tall, and because his achievements and basketball gave him an increasingly greater sense of accomplishment, Yao Ming discovered more and more how fascinating basketball was. Yao Ming has waxed poetic in describing the basketball that he loves so earnestly:

"The sounds of the court, the atmosphere of the court, bodies colliding, the sweat flying off from the impact, plus the 'swoosh' of the ball as it goes through the basket, the sound of basketball shoes scraping on the court, and the 'tick-tock, tick-tock' of the time clock as it runs, the sound of the referees' whistles — all of these are beautiful to hear! Just like a symphony."

He says, "As far as I am concerned, basketball is a part of life. Life is all, and basketball is a part of life. Basketball is a very interesting game, a game that is simple and not simple — simple because it has a certain regularity that can be followed, yet not simple because this regularity is constantly changing and sometimes cannot be grasped."

Yao Ming loves to play computer games, and he himself cannot count how many different kinds of games he has played over the years, but he has never played basketball computer games. After teaming up with the Houston Rockets, someone asked him whether he had liked the Rockets' NBA video game before that, and Yao Ming replied, "I generally don't play sports games. I feel that the basketball that I play is too wonderful, and basketball computer games are a bit lacking in flavor when compared to real basketball."

What is interesting is that at the Xu Jia Hui Youth Sports School Yao Ming also trained in water polo for a very short time, solely for amusement. He was too tall, and when his young teammates of the same age advanced in the pool, waving their arms, if he were not careful and stood up in the water, it was like a long-legged, long-necked red-headed crane suddenly charging into the midst of a bunch of ducklings ruffling their wings — but as a consequence of that short stint of water polo training, swimming became a great love of Yao Ming's from then on.

Three Bottles of Milk

Li Zhangmin, the 47-year-old basketball coach of the Xu Jia Hui Youth Sports School, is saving a photograph of Yao Ming with pursed lips amongst a group of kids practicing basketball — "a crane standing in a flock of chickens." What attracts the eye is the basketball gym in the background, its windows all cracked and broken. Li Zhangmin says that outside the basketball gym is the soccer stadium. With basketballs hitting them from inside and soccer balls from outside, it would be a wonder if the windows weren't shattered.

Yao Ming still remembers how the basketball gym used to be: concrete walls on all sides and a plastic canopy above. "Actually, you couldn't really consider it a gym." This "basketball gym," which no longer exists, used to have four earthen courts, and it was here that Yao Ming began his basketball training.

"When Yao Ming was in third grade, he started training basketball with me. That was in 1989, because Yao Ming had to start elementary school one year earlier than others his same age," Li Zhangmin says. At that time, Yao Ming's mother, Fang Fengdi, went to see Xu Weili, branch secretary at the Xu Jia Hui Youth Sports School, to find out who was the basketball coach for students Yao Ming's age. Secretary Xu said it was Li Zhangmin, and Fang Fengdi, hearing this, was completely at ease and sent her child to the school the next day.

Actually, Fang Fengdi had wanted for a long time to send Yao Ming to the Youth Sports School, but he wasn't yet old enough for her to send him to that school. When Yao Ming was in second grade at the Gao An Road First Elementary School, the teacher in charge of his class, Gong Lingzhen, paid a visit to Yao Ming's house, and Fang Fengdi vented her grievances to Teacher Gong: "Yao Ming is growing too fast. If this goes on, even sleeping will become a big problem. He eats a lot, and we don't have a big income, so it's hard to make sure he gets enough nourishment."

Gong Lingzhen remembers that when Yao Ming was little his home environment was in fact very impoverished. On the spring and fall outings, he brought only very simple things. The income of both Yao Zhiyuan and Fang Fengdi combined was not more than 100 yuan (about $12) a month — despite the fact that Fang Fengdi had formerly been captain of the national women's basketball team. After she retired, her monthly income was only about 40 yuan (or $5). The parents were both tall athletes who had always had big appetites, and now there was also a vigorously growing child; thus, the family's income all went for food. Yao Ming's aunt, Yao Zhiying, says, "My brother and sister-in-law skimped on clothing and food so that Yao Ming could eat well; they gave everything they saved to their child."

In those days, whenever she went from Zhen Ze to Shanghai, she always took chickens and eggs to improve Yao Ming's nourishment. Yao Zhiying's child, Yao Ming's cousin Qian Yao, remembers that Yao Ming could eat a whole chicken in one meal. "He loved to eat pickled eggs, and he could eat six at a time."

Jiang Jiafeng, veteran basketball reporter of the *New People's Evening Post*, was one of the first journalists to interview Yao Ming — when Yao Ming was only four years old — and he wrote an article entitled "If Yao Ming Had a Little Sister," which discussed the reasons why Yao Zhiyuan and Fang Fengdi had only one child: Someone asked jokingly of Cong Xuedi, head coach of the Shanghai women's basketball team that had tasted two defeats in a row, if the women's basketball team had a little sister of Yao Ming to look forward to, what would the situation be like then? Cong Xuedi, who had been glum-faced just a moment before, broke out laughing: "Oh, then it wouldn't be about just winning a few games; then we'd be talking about the possibility of winning the WCBA championship!"

In fact, this statement is not so fantastic after all; it's only because that time, which was just after the conclusion of the ten-year "catastrophe" when all neglected matters were awaiting resurgence, was a particular period in history when people were still filled with regret, daring to think but not daring to act. At the end of the 1970s, when Yao Zhiyuan, starting center for the Shanghai men's basketball team, and Fang Fengdi, captain of the national women's basketball team, got married, there were a lot of "idealists" who strongly urged the tallest couple in Asia to "raise" a few future stars for Chinese basketball. It is said that leaders from the authorities had talked to Big Yao and Big Fang about this, but that the matter was subsequently dropped for reasons unknown. Hearsay has it that the leaders from the authorities at that time had only given verbal approval for the expenses of raising future stars but there was no effective agreement in writing.

After they were married, Big Yao retired from the Shanghai men's basketball team and entered harbor inspection work, and Big Fang left her position as captain of the national women's basketball team to return to Shanghai and work at the Institute of Sports Science. Because both Big Yao and Big Fang had had careers as athletes, and because they were "big and tall," the two of them basically spent their wages on "meals." After Yao Ming was born, this situation — the income of two persons but expenditures for "six persons" — caused hardship for Big Yao and Big Fang. They remember that when Yao Ming was four years old, he was already 4'2". When his parents took him to the park they had to buy him a bus ticket; even to get a haircut he had to pay as an adult. While Yao Ming was growing, his appetite was especially good, and he would finish an entire 2lb dish of barbeque eel and a braised pork shoulder in one meal. In order to guarantee Yao Ming's nutrition, Big Yao and Big Fang had to deny themselves and eat less. At that time, their one-room apartment in a new housing project was too crowded for the family of Big Yao, Big Fang, and Yao Ming. A large custom-made bed occupied most of the space in the room, and of course there was no modern furniture or home appliances. Anyone tactlessly broaching the subject of nurturing a few future basketball stars with Big Yao and Big Fang would surely have been snubbed.

As an athlete, Fang Fengdi knew the importance of strengthening her son's nutrition, and by the time he was in second grade, Yao Ming was already drinking two bottles of milk each day. At that time, "milk ration tickets" were needed to buy milk, and Yao Zhiyuan and Fang Fengdi had to obtain these somehow.

But two bottles of milk was not enough to keep up with Yao Ming's nutritional needs, and the Yao family had no way to obtain a third bottle of milk — however, the students at the Youth Sports School were each provided a bottle of milk.

Gong Lingzhen consoled Fang Fengdi: "If you can just hold on for one more year, when Yao Ming begins third grade he can enter the sports school."

Li Zhangmin, who had been sent down to the countryside, later became a student in the class of 1978 in the Department of Physical Education at Shanghai Normal University. He is stable, kind and honest, and has a high level of intelligence. He remembers that when Yao Ming first started basketball training he had no basketball fundamentals whatsoever, and his cardiopulmonary functions were nothing special: he couldn't run two laps around the court, and in group drills he would get really tired right away.

When they saw Yao Ming was like this, some of the coaches

at the Xu Jia Hui Youth Sports School didn't think much of him; they thought that even though Yao Ming was tall, he wasn't really suited to train in basketball. Li Zhangmin says: "One of the coaches made a wager, that if Yao Ming could actually become a basketball player, he would quit coaching." And this coach did in fact stop coaching — by the time Yao Ming's fame shook the world, he had already retired.

But at that time, Yao Ming's sole advantage was his height. In third grade, he had already grown to 5'5", and Li Zhangmin said that children of that age who had reached 4'5" were already considered tall.

He and the Xu Jia Hui Youth Sports School's Sports Science Research team performed some tests on Yao Ming's body, and they also did bone-age determination, predicting that Yao Ming would be more than 7'2" — "What great basketball material!"

Yao Ming trained under Li Zhangmin for five years, up until he joined the Shanghai municipal youth team when he was in the second year of junior high school. Li Zhangmin put a lot of time and effort into training Yao Ming, and sometimes when Yao Ming's parents had no free time because they had to work, he would go pick up Yao Ming at the GaoAn Road First Elementary School and take him out for some practice.

"To be honest, in the beginning Yao Ming was not much interested in basketball; he was just fooling around." Li Zhangmin says, "But Yao Ming was very obedient, and he was very serious in his training; he would do whatever the trainer arranged for him to do. If I asked him to practice a particular movement twenty times, he would actually do it the whole twenty times, unlike some team members who 'cut corners'."

Besides being obedient, Yao Ming was also a sensible and

intelligent child. During one practice session, somebody came over to announce the good news that Li Zhangmin's wife had had a baby. The whole group of children was all interested to hear this, but Yao Ming was the only one who went over and asked, "Coach Li, was it a boy or a girl?" At that time, Yao Ming was only nine years old, and many of his teammates were older than he was. At the beginning of 2002, when Yao Ming's reputation had spread worldwide, he ran into Li Zhangmin, and asked, "How's your daughter these days?"

"It had been ten years, yet he still was considerate enough to ask about his beginning coach's kid!" Li Zhangmin's memory of this occasion is especially deep.

Thus the very attentive Yao Ming gradually began to display his talent for basketball. At that time, the Xu Jia Hui District Youth Sports School provided three types of meal subsidies for athletes: "top-notch," "key," and "ordinary," and although he had just joined and had the poorest skills, Yao Ming was able to get the "top-notch" subsidy, which was about 60 cents per day, right away; by contrast, the "normal" subsidy was only 12 cents per day. This was undoubtedly very important to the rapidly growing Yao Ming.

Later on, the Xu Jia Hui District Youth Sports School and the Shanghai Municipal Sports Committee reported again to the National Sports Committee that Yao Ming had limitless potential and asked for support. After the leadership of the National Sports Committee came to see Yao Ming, they made a special appropriation of 10,000 yuan (or about $1,200) to subsidize Yao Ming and the other basketball prospects. In the early 1990s, this was an "enormous sum," and Li Zhangmin says, "Yao Ming is what he is today because of the concern and solicitude of many parties."

Today, as Yao Ming is depending on his basketball skills to conquer the NBA, Li Zhangmin's critique is that although Yao Ming is tall, he doesn't rely on his height or strength to play ball; rather, he uses his brain to play ball, just like his mother used to.

But the superstar's first coach now finds himself in a vexing situation: all of the young players under his tutelage worship Yao Ming, but their academic burden is too heavy and it is difficult to guarantee enough daily training time.

"Now there is too much class work in school, and the students' burden is very heavy, with a lot of assignments, and there are all kinds of special-interest classes and remedial classes, so the training is in fits and starts, and without systematic training, how will it be possible to lay down a good foundation?" Li Zhang Min worries.

Fortunately, in those days when Yao Ming was attending elementary school, there was no notion of "lightening the burden," and although keeping up with class work was tough, it was nevertheless possible to guarantee two hours of practice every day.

"Nowadays, everyone is so busy with class work every day, and even Yao Ming would not be able to become successfully trained," Li Zhangmin says. "One of the keys to Yao Ming's success was that not a single period of 'sports sensitivity' was wasted during the various stages of his physical development. For example, the age of seven or eight is the best time to train reaction time and sensitivity, and once past this age it is too late to train these things."

Son of the Yao Family

In those days, Yao Zhiyuan and Fang Fengdi never thought that there would be a day when their own son would become a superstar.

When they were athletes, there was no concept of "superstar."

This man and wife were basketball players in the 1970s, and at that time, sports were deeply branded by politics, especially group sports like basketball, so how could the existence of the "individual" be allowed?

When they played basketball, they heard some faint mention of something called the National Basketball Association in far-off America, but at that time even in their dreams they could not have imagined that they would someday go to an NBA arena to see a game, or that they would be watching their own son playing ball in the NBA.

The sports careers of Yao Zhiyuan and Fang Fengdi were part of the "dragon" system unique to Chinese sports. The tail of the "dragon" extended into the nursery schools and lower elementary school grades, where children were initially selected when they were babies; then, these prospects left their desks and put aside their books to enter the various municipalities' youth sports schools. After an extremely high percentage were eliminated, those remaining joined various outstanding provincial and municipal sports teams and specialized sports work teams, which comprised the skeleton of the "dragon." After further elimination, the cream of the crop finally made it to the "dragon's head," that is, the national teams, where they received specialized long-term refining and polishing to represent the nation in competition until the end of their athletic careers. They had only one mission: to win gold medals — members of the national teams had to take gold in international competition, and members of provincial and municipal teams had to win gold in comprehensive sports meets.

Yao Zhiyuan only made it as far as the "dragon's body," never joining the national team, but Fang Fengdi made it to the "dragon's head" as captain of the Chinese national women's basketball team, which was the highest level that a Chinese athlete could reach at that time.

This "dragon" really did allow handfuls of Chinese athletes to attain the pinnacle in sports and win gold medals; but many ordinary athletes were trapped for years in a confined environment by this "gold medal rule" mentality, missing the chance during the best years of their lives to obtain cultural knowledge. When they retired, they found themselves at a loss, searching this way and that, not knowing what they could do or what they wanted to do.

What to do with retired athletes has always been a tough problem for China's sports program, and this is one of the main reasons why many Chinese sports families don't want their sons and daughters to go into sports. But now, as Yao Ming continues to display more and more outstanding basketball talent and excellent skills, and with his excellent prospects for the future, people admire the long-range vision of Yao Zhiyuan and Fang Fengdi. However, Yao Ming's parents originally never intended to have their son play basketball; they only wanted him to do well in his studies and be able to pass the entrance exams for a good school.

"When I told him to play basketball, I was just hoping that he would get some exercise," says Yao Zhiyuan. Even though he sent Yao Ming to the youth sports school, which was beginning the transition from the "tail of the dragon" to the "body of the dragon," he did so because he thought that being able to play basketball would prove an advantage to get into better middle schools and universities in the future.

Liu Wei, a national team player and Yao Ming's good friend on the Shanghai Sharks, has confirmed this point: he trained so hard in basketball to get into a good school later on, and he "never thought he would be a professional player."

After Yao Zhiyuan retired, he became a worker; Fang Fengdi, because of her outstanding achievement, got what could be considered a "suitable assignment" when she went to the Shanghai Sports Institute. Salaries then were very low, and most of this family's expenditures went toward meals. They lived a difficult life.

Good prospects like Yao Ming who possess extraordinary height receive more attention when they go from the youth sports schools to the youth teams. The policies of the National Sports Committee, the Shanghai Sports Committee, and the Physical Education and Sports Technical College favor these young hard-to-find players. But in those days, funds were limited because of the need to rely on financial appropriations.

Moreover, at the end of the 80s and the beginning of the 90s, the basketball scene in Shanghai was disheartening to Yao Zhiyuan and Fang Fengdi: a moribund Class-B team — even if Yao Ming were to "follow in his father's footsteps," what would he be able to accomplish? Maybe he would play ball for a few years, get injured, retire at a young age, and sink into oblivion.

Shanghai was the earliest city in the nation to start developing basketball. In the early 1950s, the level of basketball in Shanghai was fairly good, and the city was deemed the "cradle of basketball" in China. In the latter part of the 50s, the Shanghai men's basketball team was ranked third in the nation and had represented China in the World Collegiate Sports Meet, beating the strong world-champion Brazilian team. The fast and lively style of play was developed that year by those team members.

A few years later, when young players like Wang Zhongguang, Zhang Dawei, and Yang Jiaxun began to emerge, the Shanghai men's basketball team enjoyed several years of glory, playing their way to first place in the national championship — although this first place was not comparable to the CBA championship in 2002. But the glory didn't last long; when the entire nation was engulfed by the sudden tempest of the Cultural Revolution, the sports world was doomed.

At the end of the 70s and the beginning of the 80s, when Yao Zhiyuan and Fang Fengdi were at the height of their careers, Shanghai basketball began to revive and again reached a high level, ranking 3rd overall nationwide. But by the end of the 80s and the beginning of the 90s, the Shanghai men's basketball once again fell into the doldrums, its bench faltering and coaches departing one after another. At that time, although the Shanghai team still existed, only a skeleton crew was still on board. At its worst, the team of China's most imposing city dropped to last place among all the teams in the nation; to find it you had to count backwards from the end of the Class-B teams, and for a while it wasn't even eligible to compete in national sports meets.

"At that time, the players playing on business-sponsored amateur teams were making much more money than the specialized teams. The sports teams were completely passive, living on fixed income provided by the state and being paid to play ball, and at the age of 25 or 26 the players would start thinking about other options and stop thinking about playing basketball." Li Qiuping, head coach of the Shanghai Sharks, remembers with considerable regret how it was when he took over the Shanghai basketball team. The teams had little skill and accomplishment, and salaries were low.

Shanghai basketball legend Wang Zhongguang was heartbroken by basketball at one point: "After the players retired, their income was very low. My salary at my work unit was the same as a janitor's, no difference at all. There was a schoolmate of mine who took a job after finishing elementary school, and later on, when I was in the second year of junior middle school, I ran into him at the movies. That was in the summertime, and he was wearing a wristwatch, proud as a peacock — you have to realize that there were some coaches on our sports committee who had worked for ten years and still couldn't afford to buy a wristwatch."

Wang Zhongguang remembers that back then when he went into basketball, there was no way that this was his own personal choice. "In those days, there was no freedom of individual choice."

At the beginning of the 1960s, Wang Zhongguang was in high school, studying at Shanghai's then-famous Gao Qiao Middle School. His grades were very good, he dreamed of taking the entrance examination for Qinghua University or the Harbin College of Military Engineering. He was a good basketball player. But it was only an avocation, he says candidly: "In those days, athletes were looked down upon."

He never thought that he could only become an athlete, and when the higher education exams drew near and the students were to fill out their vocation forms, everyone but Wang Zhongguang had a vocation form, so he asked the teacher in charge of the class, and it turned out that the school principal was hoping that he would go to play ball for the sports work team. Wang Zhongguang obstinately went to find the principal and ask for a vocation form, but the principal disagreed: "Qinghua University? We don't value that. You go be an athlete, and win honor for Shanghai, for China!"

On July 7, the day of the higher education examinations, his classmates all went to the examination hall, but Wang Zhongguang, carrying his bedding on his back, reported to the Shanghai sports work team. Quite a few of his schoolmates of those years went on to become famous professors or well-known specialists, and Wang Zhongguang also became famous in sports, yet in reminiscing about these events of the past, he can't help sighing: "In those days, sports was too politicized; there was nothing I could do."

When Yao Ming was growing up at the beginning of the 1980s, people could already choose their own future paths. "My parents never hoped I would play basketball. They hoped that I could be the college student type and treat basketball as an amateur hobby," Yao Ming remembers.

Right at the time that Yao Ming entered the youth sports school to train in basketball, a journalist came to interview him, but Fang Fengdi would not allow it. She wasn't planning on having Yao Ming become a basketball player, and she was afraid that the reporter would put pressure on her son.

Although this couple had both come out of basketball and

were extraordinarily talented, they never had intentionally tried to foster in the young Yao Ming an interest in basketball. Yao Ming says afterwards that when he was little, "They never taught me basketball."

Yao Ming saw his father, Yao Zhiyuan, play one game at the Hu Wan Gymnasium, where he played for the Shanghai Harbor Superintendence Bureau and won runner-up in the championship. The champions were a gang of young stalwarts, and "I felt then that my father couldn't run anymore because his knee joints were bad. I watched him play that time, but felt nothing."

In 1994, when Yao Ming was thirteen and a half years old and had been training basketball at the Xu Jia Hui Youth Sports School for almost five years, he was picked by Li Qiuping to join the Shanghai youth team. By then, Yao Zhiyuan and Fang Fengdi had already accepted the fact that Yao Ming would play for a specialized team. It should be said that this was a choice based on the assumption that when conditions were ripe, success would come. Despite the fact that Yao Ming still didn't like basketball, his height of nearly 6'5" before the age of 14 made everyone feel that he ought to play basketball, and so he could only go along with this.

But there is no doubt that Yao Ming came along at just the right time, when the sports revolution was in full force. During his first year at the youth sports school the professional soccer association matches were started in twelve cities throughout the nation, and the Chinese Basketball Association was born the following year.

As natural products of the market economy, soccer and

basketball, which have huge fan bases in China, served as trail-blazers for the sports revolution, and they were necessary for the existence and development of major sports.

Before the sports revolution, China resembled the Soviet Union and the countries of Eastern Europe, with specialized state-subsidized sports but no professional sports. Prompted by various worries and other concerns, many high-level athletes often retired at the peak of their careers to do something else. In addition, in order to amass superior forces to win gold medals, the State Sports Committee devised a "gold-medal strategy," and the major sports, characterized by huge expenditure and little return on investment, were designated as first to be cut. For these reasons, after the 80s, China's three major sports lost their leading positions in Asia.

The Chinese Basketball Association league matches were different from the former championship matches under the plan of the National Committee in that they were a competitive system that was highly commercialized with profitability as the goal, market-driven, based on competition, self-supporting, fully responsible for profit or loss, self-limiting and developing, and possessing a great deal of autonomy and relative independence. In contrast to the former championship, what was produced by professional basketball was a kind of business activity upon which employees of all enterprises associated with it could rely as their business pursuit and their means of livelihood.

The CBA's most prominent feature was its commercialization, taking advantage of the commercial value and cultural value of high-level competitive basketball to participate in the commercial and cultural activities of society as well as enabling athletes to obtain high incomes by way of the basketball market. The true nature of professional basketball lies in the value exchange and value shift that occur as the sport of basketball, latent with commercial and cultural value, fulfills its service to culture.

After several years of foundering, the CBA has become a model example of success in China's sports revolution. According to statistics, in the 2001-2002 season, a total of 746,500 attendees watched live games, and attendance reached 87%, thus putting Chinese basketball in a positive cycle: as the level of basketball competition and entertainment value constantly increase, fans repeatedly return to the arenas and the positive attitude of business toward basketball surges, thus increasing the pace of organizational revolution and mechanism of transformation of basketball, contributing a positive atmosphere among the athletes and coaches, prolonging the careers of the athletes, giving rise to an unending stream of stars, increasing the competitiveness and quality of training, and obtaining good results in international competition.

Wang Zhongguang says that the CBA league matches had a very key function with regard to Yao Ming's final development. Before the CBA came into existence, there was only one strong team, the BaYi Rockets, but after the CBA permitted the importation of high-level foreign assistance players, there are now many strong teams, and this was a very important point, because the opponents who have helped Yao Ming to increase his level of play have been not one strong team but a number of strong teams. "An athlete's training and competition must be like this, the opponents must be tall, strong and fast, there have to be all kinds of high-level teams, and only through this kind of frequent confrontation could Yao Ming easily reach a higher level. If your opponent is too strong for you, it isn't much help, and too weak is also not much help, because then you become conceited and complacent . . . so Yao Ming came at just the right time, when the invigorating spring wind of revolution had begun to blow on basketball."

On January 5, 1996, Yao Ming turned 15, and he witnessed a crucial moment in Shanghai basketball history: the formal establishment of the Shanghai Sharks basketball club. With the help of high-level foreign assistance players, the Shanghai Sharks regained their Class-A status at the end of May, 1996, in Chengdu, Sichuan.

3.   Small Steps and Big Shoes

The Shanghai Hook

It is very difficult to imagine, but when Yao Ming first joined the Shanghai youth team, he had the worst technique of any of the rookie players.

In 1993, Yao Ming participated in the Shanghai municipal sports work team summer basketball training; in 1994, coach Li Qiuping of the Shanghai youth team brought him on board; and in 1995, when Li Qiuping took charge of coaching the Shanghai men's basketball team, Lu Zhiqiang assumed responsibility for the training of the youth team.

"He can't play ball; he can't even run." This is how Lu Zhiqiang, coach of the Shanghai Sharks, assessed Yao Ming, who had just joined the youth team.

"Yao Ming was puffy." Lu Zhiqiang chuckled, "He lost weight with us. When he first came, he was fat all over, but by practicing every day, his fat turned into muscle."

The days spent on the youth team were tough. There were not many games, and every day it was just constant, never-ending training. "Every day we trained four times: early-morning calisthenics, then morning, afternoon, and evening. Anyway, all day long, from morning till night, and our hair was never dry," says Liu Wei, who joined the youth team at the same time as Yao Ming.

Only four of that group of players got on a team; the other ten or more were all eliminated.

"Those who were able to become players were especially able to bear hardships," says Lu Zhiqiang. Yao Ming, Liu Wei, and the others were very sensible. They had to train, and when they trained they used their brains. "If you don't want to train, then no matter how much effort the coaches put forth, it will be of no use. Yao Ming has never been indifferent in training."

Lu Zhiqiang is 6'4" and could easily pat Yao Ming's head then; later, it became more difficult.

Yao Ming looked like a spring bamboo shoot with an overgrown head after the rain, and the coaches of the Shanghai Sharks all thought the same thing: it would not be possible to train Yao Ming in the same way that the ordinary athletes were trained; otherwise, this 'once in a hundred years' prospect would be ruined.

Wang Zhongguang later summed it up, saying that the reasons why Yao Ming turned out well were, first, that he came at a good time when the sports revolution allowed his talent to be able to be valued, explored, and most broadly manifested; and the opening of China to the outside allowed him to play at the world's highest level of basketball in the NBA when there were no longer suitable opponents at home; second, he inherited his parents' athletic talents; third, he never ceased his diligent training; and fourth, he received systematic and scientific training from a young age.

"Fang Fengdi had come to talk to us, and we discussed the question of how this child, Yao Ming, ought to be trained. At that time, we thought that because Yao Ming was growing and was especially tall, his bones would naturally be somewhat more 'tender' than other people's, and their strengthening would be very slow, so the application of major force would definitely cause problems! We coaches had to be patient, patient, and more patient; we could not rush, and we would have to pay attention to protect him and prevent him from being injured, to advance gradually step by step in the proper sequence. When I think about it now, we are all very gratified that in those days we did not act recklessly . . . in the past, too much talent was wasted by impatience in seeking success," Wang Zhongguang says.

Thus, when he first entered the Shanghai youth team, Yao Ming enjoyed "special treatment" in that he received less training than the others. When the others were doing strength training, he went to culture classes or just sat on the side resting, so the amount of his training was about half that of the others, and everybody was patiently waiting for him to grow stronger.

However, Lu Zhiqiang and Wang Zhongguang never let Yao Ming feel that he had been "put out to pasture," because the Shanghai team had formerly learned a lesson in this regard: a team member with very good physical qualifications had been placed on a low-training regimen by the coaches in order to avoid affecting his physical development, and as a result, this fellow came to believe that life on the sports work team was a breeze, and that when he had grown up and become strong, he would be able to bear a heavy training regime, so he was unwilling to endure hardship.

"Of course, Yao Ming's current success is inseparable from his own efforts; for no matter how good conditions might be, one cannot succeed without personal effort — furthermore, back then, except for his height, Yao Ming had no other advantages.

Other children in the same group were of better quality and had more ability than he did," Wang Zhongguang says. "Yao Ming was very well educated by his parents, and from a young age he has been honest, obedient, and sensible; and his receptivity is also pretty good, unlike some people who can't remember what the coach has said from one day to the next. Yao Ming is different; he has good awareness and a calm and cool head, and he likes to ponder questions, so in training he rarely makes the same mistake twice."

Actually, because of his height, Yao Ming had always trained together with players older than himself. He was the tallest of the group, but also the youngest.

Remembering those years of training, Yao Ming says, "Every time I reached a particular stage, when I had established my position on the team and become a mainstay, then right away I would be transferred to a higher-level team. Take the Youth Sports School for example: when I first went there, I was in the third year of elementary school, but I was placed directly into the older class for training. The Youth Sports School was divided into two forms or classes, one of which was the older class, where most of the players were in fifth or sixth grade, and the other was the younger class, whose players were in third grade or below. I stayed at the Youth Sports School for four years, and after I had trained for two years, all of the people in the older class except me went on to the higher-level municipal sports school. At that time, I felt that I was the oldest on the team — and just as I settled into the role of the oldest, I was transferred to a higher-level team, where I again became a bottom-level player, the youngest, the weakest one. On the youth team, I had just made it to a starting position when I was transferred again to the first team. On the first team I was the youngest, but I was too tall, and players on the first team who were four or five years older than I, grow as they might, could never match my height."

He thinks that this training with people above his age from beginning to end was a great help: "Because I was always placed in a position of looking upward from below, I was always able, by perceiving the shortcomings of others, to know my own short-comings and make up for them, and then attack others' shortcomings."

After Yao Ming went to play in the NBA, quickly transitioning from a "rookie" to a starter for the Rockets, the strength of his ability to adapt to a new environment and the completeness with which he expressed his potential astounded everybody: what was it that enabled a Chinese athlete only 22 years old, who had never played a game in the NBA and who had only been tempered in preseason training camp, to so swiftly find a firm footing in the NBA, a concentration of the world's most outstanding basketball players? Could the NBA really "touch a stone and turn it into gold?"

Wang Zhongguang always reminds himself: "Nobody has the Midas touch. Actually, Yao Ming already laid the founda-tion on the Shanghai team for the many skills that he has now successfully applied on the NBA courts!"

This senior statesman of Shanghai basketball has empha-sized the analysis of Yao Ming's skills: "Actually, his hook shot is mainly a small hook shot, and we call it a side shot. The differ-ence between it and a large hook shot is that the former is made when the hand holding the ball is already raised above the head and relies mainly on wrist strength, whereas the latter refers to the hook shot where the entire arm moves up from below with greater amplitude. Yao Ming practiced the small hook in China, but he never used it as much in CBA games as he has in the NBA, because in China, with his height he never needed this technique much. Moreover, comparatively speaking, the motion of this type of shot has a somewhat greater difficulty, and its accuracy is also correspondingly lower. But when he came to the NBA, his height advantage was not as distinct as it was in China, so when it came to the fierce struggle to score beneath the basket, the hook should be one of his better methods."

In the match up against the Indiana Pacers led by Jermaine O'Neal, Yao Ming did a classic "stutter-step pump fake" under the basket; his feet moving nimbly, he flashed past O'Neal, who was disoriented, broke out of the double-team and put the ball into the basket, and this made the best of that day's "five best shots" in the NBA. And Wang Zhongguang also sees where this came from: "This series is a fake which includes both foot and hand motions. Actually, Yao Ming had already grasped this in China, but since there is a big discrepancy in height between him and most of the other players in China, and since they have more nimble footwork than he, he relied mostly on his superior height. But when he went to the NBA, there was a corresponding increase in the height of his opponents, and his foot agility was reflected in the forward and backward movement."

Wang Zhongguang reemphasizes: "I always thought that after he went to the NBA, Yao Ming would be able to improve to such a great extent. It's not that the NBA can miraculously turn a stone into gold, or that he was magically transformed overnight. In fact, good foundations for a lot of the skills that he is now using in the NBA were gradually established earlier in

China. For example, his passing awareness was developed while a member of the Shanghai Sharks. Back then, he and I both knew that sooner or later he would move on to develop in a higher arena, and aside from practice and games, we often talked about the skills and movements in the NBA."

"When the Shanghai Hook was first made, once it was quenched, who could oppose its cutting edge?"

I Want to Wear Shoes

Sometimes, a goal that someone desperately pursues will be attained with unthinkable ease, like the 15- or 16-year-old Yao Ming, who didn't play ball to win the championship or go to the NBA; he trained his heart out solely for the purpose of obtaining a pair of shoes that fit.

"I have to work really hard and get on a team; then I won't have to worry about not having shoes to wear," Yao Ming often told Liu Wei, his roommate and good friend on the youth team in speaking about his "vast aspirations."

He had a pair of big feet that were "wildly growing" just like his body. At first, he wore his mother Fang Fengdi's shoes, and then he wore his father Yao Zhiyuan's shoes; but it wasn't long before his feet became bigger than Yao Zhiyuan's, so he had to go shopping for shoes. Yao Zhiyuan wore size 12 shoes, and the largest shoes that were available for purchase were size 14. Gradually, even these would not fit Yao Ming's feet.

All Fang Fengdi could do was to go to Beijing to ask some of her former teammates on the BaYi team for some shoes, as there were a lot of big players on the BaYi team, and they set

Small Steps and Big Shoes

some shoes aside for her. In Shanghai, where Yao Ming was on the youth team, each player could get two pairs of 'Warrior' brand shoes per year. At that time, there was a big player on the Shanghai team, and the 'Warrior' Shoe Factory had some large shoes in stock, so they brought them for Yao Ming to wear.

"In those days, after we wore out our two pairs of shoes every year, we had to buy shoes ourselves," Liu Wei recalls. He remembers that Yao Ming's shoes were covered with sewn-on patches and extremely ratty-looking, yet he was not willing to throw them away.

Even today, Yu Xiaomiao, leader of the Shanghai Sharks, heaves a big sigh when he talks about Yao Ming's shoes: "Fang Fengdi really knocked herself out so that her son could have a pair of shoes that fit." In 1996, Fang Fengdi got Zhang Mingji, a relative of hers in the United States, to buy a pair of size 17 white Nike-brand shoes, spending US$92. This pair of shoes was an extravagance for the Yao family. Yu Xiaomiao remembers that in those days, Fang Fengdi's clothes were also patched.

It could be said that the time he spent on the Shanghai youth team was the 23-year-old Yao Ming's most difficult time. The first year was tryout training, and he had no income whatsoever; the second year he began to draw a salary, but it was only 100 yuan (about $12), and he had a lot of expenses like lodging, meals, and shoes. Yao Ming recalls that 'Warrior' brand shoes cost more than 30 yuan a pair (about $3) at that time.

Thanks to Yao Ming's incomparable height, he had already attracted the attention of the Shanghai Sports Commission. As a player on the youth yeam, Yao Ming was still a training group member and had not yet been designated a regular; nevertheless, the Mei Long Training Facility where the team was located began to give Yao Ming favorable treatment and major support. When Fang Fengdi bought another pair of Nike shoes for Yao Ming from the U.S., Han Jingying, then head of the training facility, reimbursed Yao Ming for the cost of the shoes.

The Shanghai Sharks obtained the support of the Nike Corporation, but it was limited to the first-string players only. Yu Xiaomiao got in touch with Qian Anke, an employee of the Nike Corporation, to "search" for shoes for Yao Ming, and Qian rummaged through bins and boxes and finally found a big pair of blue shoes. As far as Yao Ming was concerned, the shoes didn't really fit, as they were too tight when he put them on; but Yao Ming was very satisfied nonetheless, and after he managed to stuff his big feet into this pair of "public shoes," he was absolutely delighted.

There is another very dramatic story about Yao Ming's shoes which has it that in the fall of 1996, the Nike Corporation, one of the CBA's sponsors, invited the entire Shanghai Sharks basketball team to a banquet, and as the players filed in one by one, the eyes of Telly Lutz, then in charge of the Nike Corporation's various sponsorship activities in China, suddenly lit up: Yao Ming, 16 years old, and nearly 7'2"! Lutz immediately noticed that this tall boy was wearing a pair of Adidas sport shoes. So right away he phoned Nike headquarters, and a few days later, Yao Ming received a brand-new pair of Nikes exactly the same style as those that Nike specially made for NBA star Alonzo Mourning.

In reality, in 1996 Yao Ming had already finished the process of becoming a regular, and he no longer had to worry about not being able to find suitable shoes. From then on, the Nike Corporation began to give him specially made shoes.

And it was from then on that the days of financial hardship of Yao Zhiyuan and Fang Fengdi began to draw to a close.

This couple had endured all kinds of hardships for Yao Ming. At the dinner table, they watched their son eat all the food while they went hungry. Fang Fengdi often worried: Yao Ming could finish a pork shoulder in one meal, and what would they do for the next meal?

He never had enough milk to drink, his pants were never long enough, he always complained that his shoes were too small.

Once they no longer needed to worry about their son's clothing, food, lodging and transportation, they then fell into an interminable state of suspenseful anticipation for their son.

On one occasion, Yao Ming's aunt Yao Zhiying phoned from her home in Zhen Ze to complain to her brother and sister-in-law: "I haven't seen Yao Ming for a long time."

Yao Zhiyuan and Fang Feng Di shouted, "We're in Shanghai and we haven't seen Yao Ming for a long time either!"

Yao Zhiyuan had three siblings, and his two younger brothers both had all girls. Yao Ming had an especially good relationship with his cousin Qian Yao, Yao Zhiying's son. When the older Qian Yao, who as a child had played with electric cars under the bed with Yao Ming, was preparing to get married, Yao Ming gave him a phone call: "When is the date of your wedding?" Qian Yao replied, "It's up to you — whenever you're available, we'll get married."

So this major event of Qian Yao's life was scheduled by Yao Ming to be on New Year's Day, and Yao Ming thought for sure that this would be a holiday for him. But it turned out that the national team had group practice on that day. Qian Yao was disappointed and angry, and he didn't wait for Yao Ming to be able to come to his wedding ceremony.

Yao Ming's competitive basketball career commenced with the Eighth National Games in 1997. From the CBA league matches to the Asian Championship and the Olympics, he was constantly traveling to compete in a never-ending rush of games, and he was able to return home only a few days each year. So even at the Spring Festival, he was only able to eat New Year's Eve dinner at home and then had to rush back to the team on New Year's Day. And even when he did make it home, he would often be able to lie down on his big bed for only a few minutes before the neighbors came knocking on the door in search of autographs.

Fang Fengdi was very concerned: "When he's at home, he doesn't want to disturb our work, and he doesn't want us to take turns taking off of work to be with him. He just likes to stay at home by himself and sleep. And we know that when he's with the team he could never take a nap."

Yao Zhiyuan and Fang Fengdi would always go to the major matches of the Sharks, as they could chat with their son there for a while; when Yao Ming played away games, this tall couple would take their seats in the living room right on time and happily discuss their son's defense, offense, and attitude toward the game in front of the television. Every time Yao Ming fell down, they were instantly speechless, staring intently at the television screen; for them, watching each game was one anxious moment after another.

"Although Yao Ming is very tall, he doesn't possess strong athletic ability. He relies mainly on his height, his brain, and his awareness to play ball. Yao Ming was a child with a strong sense of responsibility, and he is always very regretful of the mistakes that he makes on the court and blames them on himself. During the World Collegiate Sports Meet in 2001 in Beijing, there were a few games in which he didn't play very well, and he told me on the phone that it was because he wasn't any good, but we always tried to make him feel better," Fang Fengdi says.

From time to time during Yao Ming's basketball experience, his parents have given him pointers.

He remembers when he was still on the youth team, when the Shanghai men's basketball team had still not become a Class-A team. The three of them watched a match against the Beijing team where they used a "two towers" tactic with Shan Tao and Mengke Bateer. Yao Ming remembers that Shan Tao had this one move where he used his elbow to lift somebody up. "My mother said to me, 'You've got to learn this move; you have to learn how to use your body'. Her words really opened my eyes, so at least I've learned how to use my elbows. From then on my offensive power was stronger."

Tips like this mostly came from Fang Fengdi, Yao Ming says laughingly: "Maybe because my mother made it to the national team and my father didn't!"

In Yao Ming's mind, his parents were "the most ordinary mother and father who were always greatly concerned for me and loved me very much. Of course, just like all parents, they would also get on my nerves. If I came home real late, Mom would fix me something good to eat, and she would come into my room three times in two minutes to tell me where the toothbrush was, where the toothpaste was, where the towel was." He feels that the most precious quality his parents have taught him is honesty: "This is the most important thing, that and being kindhearted — but not blindly."

After Yao Ming went to the NBA, Fang Fengdi had already prepared her son's first stop in the United States. In the end, she took the opportunity to accompany her son, to fix his meals and make sure he ate everything. This is the longest time that the family members have all been together since Yao Ming joined the national team.

After Yao Zhiyuan accompanied his son to the United States, he returned once to Shanghai. Reporters asked him what made him the happiest during his forty days in Houston? Was it the game in which Yao Ming scored 30 points?

He thought for a second, and sighed: "No, what made me the happiest was that the three of us could spend such a long time together, eating together, taking walks together, just living together. Before, it was really hard for us to be able to enjoy the simple pleasures of family life."

Before that time, Yao Ming's parents had only been able to communicate with him by telephone, even though he was in the same city. Yao Zhiyuan says: "Before, on my birthday or his mother's birthday, or even on his birthday, he would give us a phone call, saying he wanted to hear our voices. Actually, we also longed to hear his voice. So on every such occasion, we always felt that we were very fortunate to have such a son as Yao Ming."

Body-Building Plan

Yao Ming first participated in an adult game on October 13, 1997. This was the men's basketball competition of the Eighth National Games, in which the Shanghai team faced the strong

Shandong team for the first time, and Li Qiuping put Yao Ming into the game six minutes into the first period.

The 7'2" youth, with his big head, spindly arms, and slightly bowed back and an astonished yet expectant look in his eyes, went into the game tense and excited.

"Put your hands up under the basket and control the backboard." This was Li Qiuping's assignment for Yao Ming. He didn't expect Yao Ming to play a comprehensive, all-out game, because this boy could still not stand up to contact.

Such a long-legged player standing beneath the basket posed a threat to every shot of the opposition, put a damper on the offensive and defensive rebounding of the Shandong team's dual centers, Gong Xiaopin and Ji Minshang, and increased the effectiveness of the Shanghai team's medium-range shooting. This contest was won by the Shanghai team, 50 to 48.

Wang Zhizhi encountered Yao Ming for the first time during the Eighth National Games. Not long after the game started, Wang Zhizhi received an offensive pass from a teammate and was just about to raise his hands to shoot, when unexpectedly an outstretched hand suddenly blocked the shot with a "slap." Wang Zhizhi was taken aback — the shot blocker was none other than Yao Ming. Later on, Ma Jian also had shots blocked.

But Yao Ming in the Eighth National Games was clearly young and inexperienced, and although in the campaign of Shanghai against Hebei the Shanghai men's basketball team won 65 to 57, Yao Ming played a full 40 minutes and scored 19 points, and after the game he was panting like an ox: "I can't play any more," he said.

"In those days, he had height and agility, but he was too frail and didn't have enough ball skills; he was only able to stand beneath the basket and defend, but offensively he was not a threat," recollects Lu Zhiqiang, coach of the Shanghai Sharks. Team leader Yu Xiaomiao also says that when Yao Ming first started playing, none of his teammates wanted to give him the ball, because when he had the ball it would get stolen.

Yao Ming's ability to make a showing in the Eighth National Games bolstered the hopes of the scientific and technical staff.

"At that time, I was given the mission of helping Yao Ming take part in the Eighth National Games competition, to be able to make a token appearance on the court and run up and down a few times — that's all," says Dr. Wei Guoping of the Shanghai Sports Technical Institute. Of course, it turned out that the mission was completed more successfully in that not only did Yao Ming make an appearance, he started his CBA career just one month later.

Wei Guoping is a member of the Shanghai Municipal Sports Sciences Council and an assistant researcher who has long been involved with sports nutrition and biochemical research, with expertise in evaluation of and recovery from body stimulation and fatigue. Since December of 1995, Wei Guoping has been responsible for Yao Ming's medical supervision and nutritional replacement, and the Shanghai Municipal Sports Bureau made a special expense appropriation in this regard.

"Yao Ming is tall, and for him to still be so agile is definitely related to my work," says Wei Guoping with pride.

When the 14-year-old Yao Ming joined the Shanghai youth team in 1994, he was 6'9" and weighed 220lbs, and neither his cardiopulmonary function nor his muscle strength were very strong, and the indoor frog jumps and outdoor 12-minute run seemed to really tax his strength.

"Yao Ming doesn't have gigantism, does he?" many wondered.

"Carrying out scientific observation and control of athletes' physiological and biochemical indices is very important with regard to scientific talent selection and deciding whether athletes can return to normal training the following day. In the past, the selection of athletes stopped at measuring their height, weight, and thickness of cutaneous fat, in conjunction with the coaches' experience. The search for basketball and volleyball players only paid attention to their height and neglected other aspects, and players with endocrine diseases were often chosen to be on teams. Actually, these athletes often suffered from 'gigantism' because of hyperpituitarism and the excessive secretion of growth hormones," Wei Guoping says.

Along with rapid advances in the realm of biomedicine, the task of talent selection is daily becoming more and more scientific. It is now possible to measure the size of the brain's pituitary gland, while at the same time adopting blood tests for indices of growth hormones, gonadotropin, testosterone, estradiol, and other hormones to comprehensively determine whether an athlete's growth and development fall within the normal range, and accordingly decide whether to accept or reject an athlete.

Using medical imaging technology, Wei Guoping proved that the size of Yao Ming's pituitary was within the normal range, and through examination of his blood it was found that the various indices of his growth and development were all within the normal range. "Yao Ming's great height is entirely due to heredity. He was born in a family of tall people, and his grandfather and father were both over 6'5", Wei Guoping says. "Now everybody could stop worrying."

Yao Ming's height was normal, but other indicators were not ideal. Wei Guoping has saved the body function test data for Yao Ming from that year:

On December 8, 1995, Yao Ming ran 1.6 miles in 12 minutes and did a 100 yard dash in 17 seconds; in performance testing in the winter of 1996, Yao Ming could run the length of a basketball court and back in 32.15 seconds. This was below par, and far worse than his teammate Jia Xiaozhong's 28.65 seconds.

"Yao Ming's problem is that he grew too fast. He's overly tall but not strong enough, with a degree of muscle development far lower than the ordinary person's. Plus he has a serious calcium deficiency, so his skeleton is not strong enough. He has no strength, so as soon as the training load becomes great, he can't take it. . . ."

Through body testing, Wei Guoping devised a comprehensive "plan to build Yao Ming's skeleton and muscles," to gradually increase Yao Ming's bone density and muscle quality in an orderly way.

Wei Guoping says that his scientific and technical support for Yao Ming can be summed up in this sentence: medical supervision, and adjustment and protection through nutrition and Chinese medicine. On a foundation of continuous testing of Yao Ming's body and observation of the load on Yao Ming's body and how it was borne, cardiac function was closely monitored. On the basis of an intimate knowledge of the state of Yao Ming's health, "balanced nutrition with adjustments via Chinese medicine" helped in achieving an optimal state. Especially when Yao Ming was overloaded, the special features of

Chinese medical practice and Chinese medicines were employed to eliminate muscle fatigue and achieve a good condition via adjustment. "Everything I used was entirely simple plant extracts. Yao Ming has been tested at least four times for stimulants during his play both in China and abroad these past few years, and there have been no problems whatsoever."

"At first, royal jelly was given to Yao Ming as a supplement, but at several times the normal dosage. Additional supplements of Chinese medicinal products were all administered in my office. Yao Ming has never purchased any outside health products, and everything was prepared by me personally."

Wei Guoping also especially invited Shanghai's most famous nephrologists and cardiologists to help devise a plan to strengthen Yao Ming.

Yao Ming was very cooperative in Wei Guoping's endeavors, and Wei Guoping also allowed Yao Ming to be "fully informed" with regard to the supplementation. Before administering anything, he would always first explain everything clearly to Yao Ming, telling him what were the advantages of taking something, and what it contained. Sometimes, Wei Guoping would even thumb through the thick Chinese Pharmacopoeia so that Yao Ming would completely understand what it was that he was taking.

Wei Guoping's guiding thought with regard to Yao Ming's supplementation was: gentle breeze and light rain, but absolutely no "stuffed duck"; in other words, oversupplementation was to be avoided.

Wei also provided guidance with regard to Yao Ming's diet, explaining very clearly what he should and should not eat. Before the Sharks basketball organization began to supply milk,

Wei Guoping told Yao Ming to "drink milk like you're drinking water" in order to provide calcium and protein.

"My job is to convert the athletes' training problems into medical problems. For example, when Yao Ming first joined the team he was not a high-percentage shooter, and from the coaches' perspective, missed shots might have been either a skills problem or an emotional problem, or perhaps just luck," Wei Guoping says. "But I thought that this was a nutritional problem, that Yao Ming lacked some kind of nutrient responsible for direction. Every kind of nutrient has its own unique function, this one being responsible for direction, that one for equilibrium, and another for explosive power . . . so giving something as a supplement would be advantageous for increasing his shooting accuracy."

So Wei Guoping became the one person who understood the most about Yao Ming's "ins and outs," and even though Yao Ming might be far away, he can tell at a glance what kind of shape Yao Ming's body is in. "Yao Ming has a customary way of moving on the court. He doesn't stand there and rest as most other athletes do; he arches his back and pants with both hands on his knees. When I see this, I know he's tired."

When Yao Ming first went to the NBA, for a time he was unable to adapt to the degree of athleticism. By the time he had played 29 regulation games, he became severely overtaxed and his shooting percentage plummeted. Fortunately, Yao Zhiyuan just at that time returned to Shanghai and made a special trip to visit Wei Guoping; then he returned to Houston with a big batch of Wei Guoping's nutrients.

Sure enough, Yao Ming's shooting percentage soared.

4. Displaying Talent for the First Time

Little Big Yao

Sports is sometimes a lot like the life of itinerant entertainers, with the ups and downs of the rich and powerful, the rags to riches stories, resentment and retribution, the showdowns between towering rivals. Naturally, there is also the creation of absolute masters.

The story of the rise of a great warrior often has a commonplace beginning. Yao Ming loved to read *Legend of the Eagle-Shooting Heroes*, when Guo Jing was still a simple shepherd and the Seven Eccentrics of the South seemed so awesome. Then there is Qiu Chuji, who appears to already have become a great warrior surpassing all others, and later on the "Black Wind Twin Goblins" and "Nine Dark Skeleton Claws" — surely the most awesome martial achievement on earth.

Nobody knew Guo Jing's future. First he got tossed around by the little Daoist priest Yin Zhiping, and later on Yang Kang beat him so that his nose was black and blue and his face swollen.

So the times always make men sigh with emotion. Guo Jing finally strides forward toward the master of the first rank.

On November 23, 1997, the 17-year-old Yao Ming played for the first time in the Chinese Basketball Association.

Before the game, there was a home-court ceremony to open the new season. In 1997, the Shanghai Sharks' home court was still at the Hong Kou Gymnasium, and when this skinny 7'2" guy came leaping out of the mouth of the big shark that was the team's mascot under the converging beams of the spotlights, a cheer swept through the audience, and Yao Zhiyuan and Fang Fengdi applauded until their hands were red. Later on, whenever the Sharks played a home game, this couple would always arrive at the court on time and, bursting with pride, watch their son from far away. But in the very beginning they were anxious.

Yao Ming's opponents in his first CBA game were the Air Force's Mighty Eagles team, and he became the starting center in the new lineup that Li Qiuping was bravely trying, the other four players being the 6'5" Lithuanian foreign assistance player Vaidas Jurgilas, Li Jian, Zhang Wenqi, and Zhang Yong.

"Number 15, Yao Ming!" Hearing this, he got up and, slapping the palms of his coaches and teammates one by one, went onto the court. The basketball audience in Shanghai was not very large at that time, but from that moment on, he was a starter for the Shanghai Sharks.

The Sharks won this game, 63 to 57. Vaidas Jurgilas scored first, and high-scorer Liu Tie of the Air Force team was firmly shut down. Yao Ming stood beneath the basket, waving a pair of gigantic hands and energetically blocking the opponents' attacks. He was still not old enough and did not have enough experience, and he was clearly not strong enough, frequently being firmly pushed out from under the basket by stronger opponents and losing his advantageous offensive and defensive positioning.

After the game, the media nicknamed Yao Ming "Little Big

Man," and during the Eighth National Games he was called "Little Long Legs" — both very neutral descriptions of his tall and slender body. This was a long time before he came to be called "Little Giant."

On November 26, the Sharks hosted the Jiangsu Dragons, winning by a narrow margin of 84 to 81, and it was in this campaign that the Sharks began to realize Yao Ming's prowess.

The Sharks' starting lineup was still Yao Ming, Zhang Wenqi, Vaidas Jurgilas, Li Jian, and Zhang Yong, and when the whistle blew, Zhang Yong quickly penetrated the opposition's hinterland and immediately threw a high pass, and Yao Ming, taking the hint and quickly seizing an advantageous position, caught the ball and smoothly put the ball in the basket, thus beginning the first half of the game with beautiful teamwork. The Sharks mainly played a lively and animated inside game, but unfortunately their scoring percentage was too low, and in the first half they trailed 36 to 37. At the start of the second half, the Sharks' play was somewhat chaotic, and the score became 37 to 45 as the opposition pulled away. Then Li Qiuping put Yao Ming back in again, and the entire team recollected itself and put all its effort into a counterattack to close the gap.

Charlie Mand, an American foreign-assistance player on the Jiangsu team, had strong individual penetration, and right away he jumped up beneath Yao Ming's giant hands for a two-handed dunk, which drew a cheer from the audience. This was the first time that Yao Ming had faced stiff opposition from a foreign player, but he showed no fear at all; instead, he grew even more excited. The Sharks set up an offensive play, which consisted mainly of the guards forcefully penetrating to disrupt the opponents' defense and create an opportunity either for Yao Ming inside or Zhang Wenqi and Vaidas Jurgilas outside to shoot and score. As center, Yao Ming was not only able to screen and support his teammates forward and backward, left and right, but he could also actively take the ball and dared to attack one on one. Many times when the opposing center forced his way to the basket, Yao Ming either blocked him or pushed for position, and Mand began to have a harder and harder time of it.

With 50 seconds left in the game, Yao Ming was one on one beneath the basket, and with two successive spin moves he broke free of his opponent and stepped toward the basket to score. Li Qiuping effusively praised Yao Ming: "Yao Ming wasn't afraid, and he made a good showing."

On November 30, 1997, the Sharks traveled to Dong Wan in Guangdong province, where they defeated the Guangdong Tigers 83 to 78 and Yao Ming scored 20 points and had 10 rebounds, his personal best in the CBA. In that game, Yao Ming was still a starter, and the Sharks led at the half 41 to 36. In the second half, after the Tigers caught up to tie the score at 60, Li Qiuping called a time-out, and he arranged for guard Zhang Yong to keep dribbling for penetration in order to create a scoring opportunity for Yao Ming on the inside, intending to utilize Yao Ming's height advantage and determined to make an inside play in order to force the opposition to tighten their defense. This was a great plan, and in order to protect under the basket, the Tigers were hesitant to launch an attack, which enabled the Sharks' mid-range outside shots to be effective, and they finally won the game.

After three CBA games, Yao Ming seemed to gradually be coming into his own, but the strongest opponent of his life was coolly waiting not far away: Yu Leping, 30 years old, 7'0", and 297 lbs.

On the evening of December 3, 1997, at the Shanghai Hong Kou Gymnasium, the Shanghai Sharks faced the Zhongxin team from Zhejiang.

Li Qiuping sent out Yao Ming, Vaidas Jurgilas, Zhang Wenqi, Zhang Yong, and Li De'en, who usually didn't play much but who was very fast, intending to take the opposition by surprise with a combination of height and speed. But the center for the Zhongxin team, Yu Leping, used his weight and height to keep Yao Ming in check.

Yu Leping's style was that of a power player, hearty and forceful. He had 286 rebounds, and he had won the title of "rebound king" in the national class-A league matches in 1995-1996. He was less than 2" shorter than Yao Ming but 66 lbs heavier, and much stronger. Yao Ming was to experience misery for the first time in his short basketball career.

"Blam!" "Blam!!" "Blam!!!"

In this game, Yao Ming was knocked head over heels 15 times by Yu Leping. At the end of the first half, the score was 25 to 26, with the Sharks trailing by one point. Twelve seconds before the end of the second half, the Sharks' Li Ye made two of two free throws, and the score was 53 to 52 as the Zhejiang Zhongxin team launched its final offensive drive. After getting the ball in the free-throw lane, Yu Leping bumped Yao Ming away, stepped toward the basket and shot, and the ball went in at the sound of the buzzer, 54 to 53. Yao Ming lost, and the Sharks also lost.

The Sharks lost because they relied too much on Yao Ming's height, and Yao Ming lost in his first attempt to defend against a big center. In the three previous games he had felt pretty good and had had a clear height advantage, but his hands were tied when he ran into the rough-and-tumble Yu Leping, and was unable to defend against him.

Encountering BaYi

After hosting and losing to the Zhejiang Zhongxin team, the Sharks immediately won two victories: first was an away game in which they defeated the Sichuan Pandas 79 to 64, a big battle between Yao Ming and the 6'9" Sichuan center Deng Guoyou in which Yao Ming was completely unfazed, went to the basket inside, got a lot of offensive rebounds and put on quite a show; the media acclaimed, "Huge blocks like swatting flies." Next was a home game in which they routed the Shenyang Armed Forces Lions 88 to 56, and after the game, Wei Gang, the head coach of the Shenyang Lions, sighed, "If only the Sharks didn't have Yao Ming guarding the inside."

But the cavalry of the BaYi Rockets would soon pulverize Yao Ming's fleeting happiness.

December 15, 1997 is a day that Yao Ming will not forget for a long time, for it was on this day at Shanghai's Hong Kou Gymnasium that the Sharks lost spectacularly to the Rockets, 66 to 106.

Yao Ming and Zhang Wenqi, Vaidas Jurgilas, Liu Wei, and Li Jian started. The Rockets' Liu Yulian was injured and out of the lineup, but all of their top players like Wang Zhizhi, Zhang Jinsong, and Ah Dijiang were in their lineup. The two teams were matching speed against speed and using height to control height. The players were in a tight man-to-man defense, and Wang Zhizhi, center for the Rockets, flashed past Yao Ming for a two-handed dunk to start the scoring, followed by a three-pointer from forward Zhang Jinsong, which made the score 5 to 0 in favor of BaYi. Despite this strong initial burst, the Sharks rapidly caught up. During the first six minutes, the score was very close, and it was hard to tell who had the advantage.

But after six minutes, the situation took a turn for the worse as the range of the Rockets' press defense gradually expanded and blocked the Sharks' "shipping lanes" both inside and outside. The Sharks took many blind shots or made passing errors, and after the Rockets got the rebounds, they seized the opportunity for fast breaks to widen the score. When Li Qiuping called time-out at six and a half minutes, the Rockets were already leading 17 to 10.

The Sharks switched often between man-to-man and zone, and they even put in their American foreign-assistance players to play "dual-centers" in coordination with Yao Ming, strenuously protecting their inside offensive ability and superiority on the boards. But now the BaYi team was firing on all cylinders, and except for Ah Dijiang, their players were all clicking, both inside and outside, and even Wang Zhizhi got a three-point shot from the perimeter. In the first half, the Sharks trailed 28 to 46; in the second half, the Sharks were completely demoralized and went crashing down to defeat: at ten minutes into the third period, the score had already become 49 to 79, and the BaYi team was simply unstoppable. The BaYi team finally concluded the contest with a full-court press and emerged with a 40-point victory.

Fifty-eight days later, the Sharks traveled west to the city of

Chongqing, where they challenged BaYi in an away game; this was the eighteenth regulation game of the season.

Li Qiuping was not expecting much: "We come here today as students. All we want to do is to play our best, and a minor loss will be a victory."

Yao Ming started this game with a calm heart; it was the Rockets' Wang Zhizhi who was upset.

Wang Zhizhi's past was like Yao Ming's present. In 1998, this 6'9" boy from Beijing was steeped in the good fortune of "total adulation."

Wang was born into a basketball family, and at the age of eight he was 5'2"; in 1991, the 15-year-old Wang had already grown to a height of 6'7", and it was in that year that he joined the BaYi Rockets, the strongest of China's domestic teams. In 1994, the 17-year-old Wang Zhizhi was selected to join the Chinese men's basketball team, becoming the youngest player ever to be on the national team in the history of Chinese men's basketball. In 1995, 1996, and 1997, he was the CBA "block king" for three seasons in succession, and in 1996 he was the first Chinese player ever selected for the World Youth All-Star team. He also won the 1996 Asian Youth Basketball Championship and MVP in 1996 and scored eighth place at the 1996 Summer Olympic Games in Atlanta.

Wang was accustomed to being the leader, and he regarded the other players with disdain, as no-one could compete with him — at least until Yao Ming showed up.

From the first day that Yao Ming set foot on the court in the CBA, public opinion never ceased to heap exaggerated praise on him. He was called "young genius," "the second Wang Zhizhi," and even "the number one center in Chinese basketball," which led to the many centers in the CBA all taking pleasure in upsetting Yao Ming in competition, and Wang Zhizhi even more so — Yao Ming had blocked his shot at the Eighth National Games before even playing in the CBA.

"Teach the boy a lesson!" Every time they played the Sharks, Wang Zhizhi's blood would boil when he saw Yao Ming, who was only two years his junior.

The Rockets put their entire first-string lineup in as starters in the contest, and they got 6 points right away. But the Sharks showed no weakness, and they were holding their own with the score at 6 to 6. Due to the tight, stubborn man-to-man defense of the Sharks, the Rockets' offense was clearly not as sharp as before.

Wang Zhizhi put all his effort into how to cope with Yao Ming. Yao Ming's strength, experience and skills were no match for his, but Yao Ming's height gave him the advantage, making Wang Zhizhi fail at several attempts to dunk.

Wang Zhizhi became impatient and could think only of besting Yao Ming. He became reckless and completely forgot the coach's pre-game strategy.

At 10:30 into the game, the Sharks took the lead for the first time, 22 to 21. Then Li Qiuping ordered the players to switch to a zone defense, and the entire team cooperated very closely, scoring time after time. At 30 to 21, the Sharks led by a considerable margin.

Wang Fei, the head coach of the Rockets, looked worried. At 13 minutes into the game, he took Wang Zhizhi out to let him cool off and calm down, and he applied a "killer" full-court press, but Li Qiuping reacted right away, changing the lineup by putting in a foreign-assistance player to cooperate with Yao

Ming, forming a dual-center formation to control the boards. At the end of the first half, the Sharks led 48 to 40.

Wang Zhizhi did not play in the second half of the game, and naturally the Sharks, which now held an absolute height advantage, locked up the area beneath the basket, and foreign-assistance player Vaidas Jurgilas used his individual ability to rush and penetrate left and right to confuse and destroy the Rockets' defense, while the BaYi players could only continue to attempt long shots to try and even the score. Although the teams were tied 64 to 64 with 9:40 remaining in the game, the Sharks took the lead right after that due to their slight advantage. Forty seconds before the end of the game, the Rockets had come back to lead by one point, 82 to 81. Then Yao Ming made a strong attack under the basket, the other team fouled, and at this key juncture, with 23 seconds remaining in the game, Yao Ming made two for two.

At the final buzzer, the Sharks finally realized that they had defeated the BaYi Rockets.

This was the first time that the Sharks had ever beaten BaYi since joining the CBA, and the following day, all the media were shouting, "Shanghai Men's Basketball Explodes Major News!"

Of course, the Rockets were very dejected by the loss, and after the game, a reporter asked Wang Fei why he didn't use Wang Zhizhi for most of the game.

Wang Fei answered stiffly, "I don't want to comment right now!"

A spirit of team unity had always been the glorious tradition of the BaYi Rockets, and it was also an important and valuable asset in overcoming the opposition and creating victory. On the BaYi team, no matter whether it was a big-name star or a young player, everyone had to put the interests of the team first.

Afterwards, Wang Zhizhi actively conducted a thorough investigation and reflected upon his personal feelings and conduct.

The game in Chongqing laid the foundation for later match-ups between the Sharks and the Rockets and gave Yao Ming's confidence a large boost.

There is no legend that cannot be defeated.

There is no shot that cannot be blocked.

Forming the Battle Lines

The Shanghai Sharks came in sixth in the 1996-1997 season and fifth in the 1997-1998 season, but the move up the ladder was extremely difficult.

The year 1997 saw major personnel turnovers in the Sharks, and a group of young native Shanghai players was in the process of changing the team's history of relying on foreign-assistance players, be they Chinese or other ethnicity. The Chinese assistance player Liang Da, who had accomplished so much the season before, as well as a group of veterans including Mao Haibin and Shao Liangen that had enabled the Sharks to rise from a Class-B to a Class-A team, left the team one by one, and there was an infusion of new blood. Of the twelve members of the Sharks, five had come from the youth team: in addition to the 17-year-old Yao Ming, there were Liu Wei, age 17, 6'1"; Li Jian, age 21, 6'3", Jia Xiaozhong, age 19, 6'6"; and Shen Wei, age 19, 6'5".

This put Li Qiuping on the spot.

On the one hand, he was tormented by doubt: if Yao Ming and the other youngsters couldn't play, then what? The Shanghai team had been a class-A team for more than a year; would its ranking fall again? On the other hand, he was surrounded by such criticism as "tearing down the bridge after crossing the river." The parents of the older players whom he had asked to retire could not understand, and they took Li Qiuping directly to task: "You needed them in the beginning when you had just taken over the team, and you said how good things would be in the future. The youngsters listened to you, and that's why they stuck around. But now that things have taken a turn for the better, now that they have helped you weather the hardships, now that life has just gotten a little bit better, you don't need them any more and you kick them out. So what's with that?" Even now, some of the parents won't speak to Li Qiuping.

After the Shanghai Sharks rose from a class-B to a class-A team in 1996, they still relied on foreign assistance players to remain competitive. As far as Shanghai men's basketball was concerned, the importation of foreign-assistance players no doubt had many benefits with regard to reorganizing and regrouping, but as the team played league matches, numerous deficiencies were also discovered: one was that the players' achievements were not stable and consistent, rising and falling as the foreign-assistance players came and went; moreover, the foreign-assistance players had an "I'm only here temporarily" attitude, and in both practice and competition they behaved like "short-timers," which was not advantageous for managing the team. In addition, retaining foreign-assistance players affected the commitment to local basketball as well as the maturation and investment in local young players.

"If we want to shake up Shanghai basketball, we have to nurture local Shanghai players," Li Qiuping said, and that year the club leadership and the coaching squad came to an agreement and made a decision: short-lived discomfort was better than long-lasting discomfort, so the 1997-1998 season would emphasize the training of new players, and with the prerequisite that the players' achievement not be allowed to slide, they would be given more time on the court.

But before one wave subsided, another arose. After several matches, Yao Ming had taken so many tumbles that everyone in Shanghai was trembling in alarm, and Li Qiuping found himself again beset by criticism: Yao Ming was so young, and making him a first-stringer was like pulling up a sprouting plant to make it longer.

At that time, a very influential article pleaded:

"When Shanghai basketball people talk of Yao Ming, everybody gets excited that such a seldom-seen 'little giant' would show up in Shanghai and that he was a local product; everybody said that with him and his teammates, Shanghai should be in the catbird seat at the Ninth National Games in another four years, and if everything were managed correctly, he will sooner or later represent the national team to play in the Olympics and the World Championship. But besides this joy there is also the worry that outsiders' hopes for him are too high; some regard him as 'Shanghai's Wang Zhizhi'. However, Yao Ming is, after all, only 17 years old and still a child, seemingly unable to bear such a heavy burden of training and competition and unable to withstand the strong resistance of his adult opponents. The next three years will be the key period for determining whether or not Yao Ming will be able to make it. With a view toward nurturing a world-class basketball player and prolonging his sports career, things must be done in a gradual and orderly progression, adopting protective measures for his training and competition. This is something that all parties concerned, including his current coaches, should have thought about before. Yao Ming needs overall protection to avoid becoming just a flash in the pan."

Yao Ming needed to mature in the fierce flames.

In fact, whenever Yao Ming took a tumble on the court, Li Qiuping was very worried off the court.

"Shanghai basketball needs Yao Ming, and if he is not allowed to grow accustomed to the atmosphere of big CBA matches as soon as possible, if he is not taught at the right time, before his skills, tactics and awareness have matured, then in another few years it will be too late." Li Qiuping remembers that he said jokingly, "During those years, no matter how thick-skinned and brazen I might have seemed, I could only bide my time in the revolutionary ranks, waiting for Yao Ming and the other young stalwarts to mature."

Li Qiuping withstood this crisis of confidence, and Yao Ming emerged after surviving the difficulties of the growth process.

From the perspective of basketball nationwide that year, it was the right time for the 17-year-old Yao Ming to go to the CBA.

In 1997, Chinese men's and women's basketball slipped considerably, both falling to third place in Asia, and the men's team even lost the opportunity to play in the World Championship. The sad state of Chinese basketball was reflected directly in that season: the level of league matches was low, and in many of the games teams were often seen to score only 50 points per game or 20 points per half; offense was weak, and "relying on defense to win" became the general rule. The players lacked enthusiasm, the veterans had spirit but no strength, and the newcomers' strength was sparse. The whole basketball market had fallen into the doldrums, and in the entire season consisting of 132 games, the only worthwhile matches were the two in which the Shandong Flaming Bulls and Shanghai Sharks had defeated the Rockets.

There were various reasons why basketball was no fun to watch: First, because the Eighth National Games didn't finish until the end of October 1997, leaving only a little more than a month for preparation before the opening of the league matches at the end of November. The resultant preparations in all areas were inadequate, especially for the players, who played two big matches back to back, leaving no time for readjustment before going back to the regular season. Second, the Center for Basketball Management of the National Sports Bureau was not established until November of 1997, and a certain amount of time was required for the turnover of tasks from the old to the new basketball management apparatus, so for a while "all the dragons were without heads." Third, some clubs blindly and hastily replaced their head coaches, which greatly weakened the effective power of some of the teams and created a decrease in the overall performance level. According to statistics, 8 of 12 teams replaced their head coaches, and among these, the Sichuan Pandas replaced its head coach again in the middle of a league match, a phenomenon that is unprecedented and will never happen again in Chinese basketball. Fourth, the level of foreign-assistance talent was generally worse than in the previous season.

But an even more fundamental reason was that the basketball management apparatus of the past never developed a group of superior coaches. Seemingly, all the coaches were blindly giving orders during league matches; moreover, nobody emphasized training and competition for the second-string players, and this created a temporary shortage of talent in Chinese basketball. Sports teams at the various levels were beset by many problems in the utilization of personnel, and the serious after-effects thus produced would continue to plague basketball for the next couple of years.

So of course in those lackluster times, Yao Ming became a marvel.

Best Practices

At the conclusion of the 1997-1998 season, the Sharks won fifth place, and Yao Ming received a "sports ethics award."

Except for getting second place in this award during the current season for 45 blocked shots — Wang Zhizhi held first place with 74 blocked shots — Yao Ming most of the time seemed like a young beginner with little achievement who was simply observing the expert older players boisterously jostling with one another to determine the ranking order among the season's heroes.

Yao Ming's first CBA season was a wash-out: the champion was still the BaYi Rockets, with the Liaoning Hunters second and the Shandong Bulls third; the Shenyang Army Lions and the Sichuan Pandas were demoted to Division II. The best lineup was center Wang Zhizhi (BaYi), forwards Gong Xiaobin (Shandong) and Hu Weidong (Jiangsu), and guards Li Xiaoyong (Liaoning) and Wei Wen (Guangdong).

In the individual skills statistics, the "points king" was Gong Xiaobin with 604 points, and he was also that season's MVP; the "three-point king" was Zhang Jingdong with 61; "rebound king" was Mengke Bateer with 226; "slam-dunk king" was Wang Zhizhi with 41; "block king" was Wang Zhizhi with 74; most assists was Li Xiaoyong with 117; and most steals was Ju Weisong.

As for the Sharks' statistics, not only did they retain the title of first in blocked shots with an average of 4 per game (tied with BaYi), they also averaged 35 rebounds per game, winning first place in that team category, which was a great improvement over the results of the previous season, when the team placed only eighth (with 28). However, they also garnered the dubious distinction of being tied (with the Zhejiang team) for first place in turnovers, averaging 16 per game.

Enthusiasm and turnovers, tenacious struggle, and a dearth of experience pretty much summed up Yao Ming's first CBA season.

With 22 pre-season games plus three quarter-final games, Yao Ming got quite a workout. Sometimes he did very well, his pair of giant hands covering the sky beneath the basket and completely frustrating the opposition; other times, the opposition held him in an offensive position and he seemed to be hapless, making a lot of turnovers in passing and grabbing few rebounds — then the opponents would quickly widen the score.

During his first season, Yao Ming had a lot of very memorable matches.

On January 14, 1998, the Sharks beat the Zhejiang Zhongxin team 61 to 50, and Yao Ming, who in the previous game had been knocked for a loop 15 times by the Zhejiang center Yu Leping, did not allow the opponents to burn him for the second time by "grabbing his jersey and throwing him down."

He had learned his lesson from the loss the last time and did his best to keep Yu Leping outside the lane, shutting down his strong attack beneath the basket, and the Sharks' outside players froze out shooter Chen Zhiming of the Zhejiang team. In the first half, the Sharks led 33 to 17, and in the second half, Yao Ming played a dual-center formation to control the boards. After 17 minutes, when Yao Ming, who had been going all-out against Yu Leping, fouled out, the Zhejiang team put on an inside offense and went on a 9-point run, so Li Qiuping adjusted the lineup right away and used a "three-short, two-tall" formation against the opposition to maintain the lead until the end of the game.

It was in this match that Yao Ming began to understand the subtleties of playing smart.

On February 15, 1998, four days after their sudden and unexpected victory over the Rockets in an away game, the Sharks lost 73 to 76 to the Shandong Bulls. This defeat was closely linked to Yao Ming.

The Sharks had utilized their slight advantage to defeat the Shandong team in the Eighth National Games, and they won by a narrow margin over the Rockets in a league match on the road. The entire team was emotionally charged for this match-up at home.

The starting lineups for both teams used all the top players. The Sharks' Zhang Yong broke through for a lay-up to open the scoring, and then the Shandong team's Gong Xiaobin followed suit with a strong inside attack. Because the Sharks' offense was for a time rash and impetuous, they missed shot after shot, and the steady Shandong team took advantage of the opportunity to rapidly increase their score. So the Sharks put in Yao Ming as a dual center, but they still trailed 27 to 35 at the conclusion of the first half. The Shandong team also paid the price of Gong Xiaobin committing four fouls. In the second half, Gong Xiaobin didn't start, and the Sharks attacked inside and shot from the outside in a frenzy. Li Ye put on a valiant show, sinking three-point shots left and right. At four minutes, the Sharks caught up to tie the score at 37 all, and then they went ahead 40 to 39. The Shandong team saw that things weren't going their way, and they sent in Gong Xiaobin. The two sides went from 56 all to 65 all. Twenty-seven seconds before the second-half buzzer, the Shandong team's Gong Xiaobin made two out of two free throws and it was 65 all, and the Sharks still had enough time to successfully put together an offensive play. Also, at this point both teams had seven team fouls, so it was a prime opportunity for the Sharks: all they had to do was to control the clock and have someone break free under the basket for a lay-up, and even if they couldn't get the ball in, it was very likely that the other team would commit a foul and they would end up winning by a free throw.

While Zhang Yong was dribbling to kill the clock, the other team members seemingly were unable to get going, so Zhang Yong hastily passed the ball to Yao Ming, but before Yao Ming had control of the ball, it was stolen by the Shandong team in the confusion. The failure of the Sharks' offensive play at this critical juncture sent the game into overtime. During the first two minutes of the five-minute overtime, the Sharks led 73 to 69, but then the experience of the Shandong team finally came into play, and they pulled themselves together. Gong Xiaobin stormed the basket and scored on an interception and dunk, and the teams were tied at 73 all. This was the eighth time that the game was tied. During the final 30 seconds, Yao Ming missed two free throws and thus an opportunity to take the lead, and in the desperate, final scramble the Shandong team knocked the ball out of bounds at the baseline, giving the Sharks yet another opportunity to go on the offensive. But they turned the ball over while passing and it fell into the hands of the Shandong team, who came back during the final four seconds of play, with Ju Weisong's pull-up jump shot from outside the three-point line going into the basket at the buzzer.

After the game, Li Qiuping said, "When the game gets to this stage, every time on offense is a critical time, and every turnover is deadly." From their previous victory over the Rockets to this sad loss, Yao Ming came to deeply understand his own immaturity and instability. Against stiff opposition it was all too easy to let the key moments slip away.

21. *Using the internet to keep updated on news and events (Li Yue / Xinhua).*

22. *Listening to the results of the NBA draft via satellite feed, June 2002. Yao Ming's parents are to his left and his coach, Wang Fei, sits to his right (Chen Xiaowei / Xinhua).*

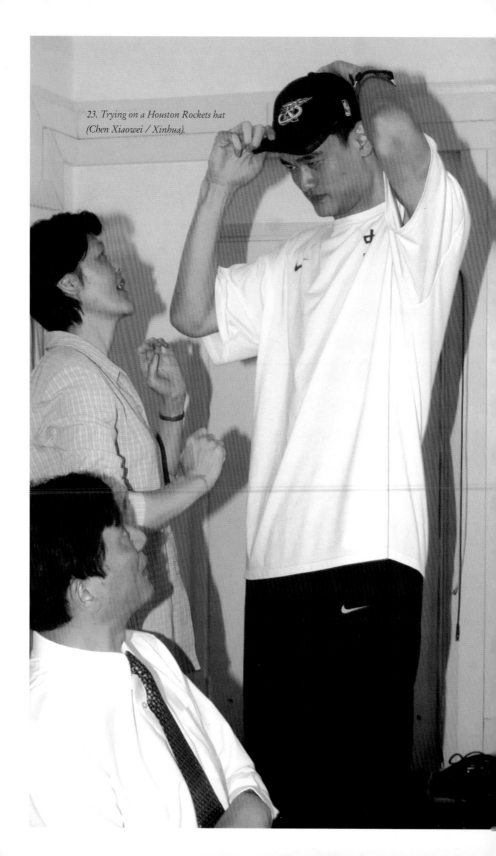

23. Trying on a Houston Rockets hat (Chen Xiaowei / Xinhua).

24. *Visiting his Alma Mater: attracting young fans outside the Gao An Road First Elementary School in Shanghai (Author photo).*

26. *Looking back in a moment of reflection (Author photo).*

25. *Before leaving for the U.S., Yao Ming visits his first teacher, Gong Lingzhen (Author photo).*

27. *Leaving Shanghai with his father, Yao Zhiyuan (Author photo).*

28. ~ 29. Yao Ming and the Houston
Rockets in a match against the Los
Angeles Clippers (Li Yue / Xinhua).

30. ~ 33. In a match against the Denver Nuggets. With Steve Francis; Yao and Nené (Hilario) go for a rebound; Marcus Camby goes up to block Yao Ming (Li Yue / Xinhua).

34. Yao Ming's Shanghai Sharks #15 jersey is officially retired on January 5, 2003. Yao became the first player in Chinese professional sports to have his number retired (Author photo).

35. Passing out autographed basketballs to thank the members of the Shanghai Military Medical College who are en route to Beijing during the outbreak of SARS in the Summer of 2003. Pictured with him is Sun Wen of the Chinese women's soccer team. Note Yao's "Jordan 23" windbreaker (Jing Wei / Xinhua).

5.   Outstanding Years

Great Joy, Great Sorrow

With expectation there often comes disappointment. The first major setback that Yao Ming encountered was when he was not chosen for the Asian Games lineup in 1998.

Had Yao Ming not previously been chosen for the overall lineup of the national collective training team, he probably would not have taken not being chosen so hard.

On March 20, 1998, the Chinese Basketball Association announced the all-star team roster as chosen by the fans and the news media for the 1997-1998 season, and Yao Ming, who had played in the CBA only for the first time, was awed to find his name on the list.

The Chinese players chosen for the all-star team lineup were: Wang Zhizhi (BaYi), Gong Xiaobin (Shandong), Li Xiaoyong (Liaoning), Hu Weidong (Jiangsu), Mengke Bateer (Beijing), Wu Naiqun (Liaoning), Ju Weisong (Shandong), Zhang Jinsong (BaYi), Ji Minshang (Shandong), Li Nan (BaYi), Yao Ming (Shanghai), and Liu Tie (Air Force).

On April 4, 1998, the CBA All-Star Game was held in the northern city of Shenyang, and due to the long shot made at the last second by the American foreign-assistance player Ray Kiely of the Sichuan Panda team, the foreign all-star team made up of a bunch of second-string European and American basketball players defeated the Chinese all-star team 83 to 80.

Yao Ming was on the court for only a short time, spending most of the time on the bench. In the bleachers, fans kept pointing him out: "Look, that's Yao Ming – he's only 17, but I hear he's already 7'2"!" "He's got a great future ahead of him!"

He was perturbed and uneasy. Before the game, somebody quietly told him, "You made the overall collective training roster of the national team."

"Don't kid me." He didn't believe it, but his heart was wild with joy.

After the game was over, Li Yuanwei, then vice-chairman of the National Sports Bureau's Basketball Sports Management Center, announced the collective training roster, and only then did Yao Ming dare believe his ears.

The newly-established Chinese Men's Basketball Collective Training team was headed by the BaYi Rockets' coach, Wang Fei. The coach was Zhang Bin of the Jinan Military Region team. The sixteen players on the team were Mengke Bateer (Beijing), Yao Ming and Zhang Wenqi (Shanghai), Li Xiaoyong and Wu Naiqun (Liaoning), Gong Xiaobin and Ju Weisong (Shandong), Sun Jun (Jilin), Hu Weidong (Jiangsu), Ding Wei (Guangdong), and Wang Zhizhi, Liu Yudong, Li Nan, Zhang Jinsong, Liu Qiang and Ah Dijiang (BaYi).

The 17-year-old young man did not know how to express the joy in his heart, so he strode back and forth by himself in the hotel lobby, oblivious to the curious stares of the hotel staff; whenever he bumped into someone he knew, he would answer, "I'm just taking a stroll."

He was so excited! He wanted to find a quiet spot to mull

over the news, to digest being chosen for the first time to join the national team. That evening, it happened that Wang Zhizhi had a fever, and Yao Ming said, "I'll go buy you some medicine." So he went out by himself.

At the beginning of April, the night in Shenyang had a bitterly cold wind, but Yao Ming didn't feel cold at all as his excitement propelled him to walk the empty streets.

To be selected to the national team had been his dream ever since he joined the Shanghai youth team. His parents' glory and dreams of traveling the country to play basketball, and their disappointments and regrets, had been passed to him along with his inherited basketball talent and were flowing in his blood; they had lay dormant for a number of years, but now they had suddenly awoken on this chilly spring night.

"I've got to calm down, calm down, CALM DOWN!" He let the wind blow across his burning forehead, and he admonished himself to work hard after he joined the national team. Now that things were just getting started, he didn't want to experience the regrets of his father of not actually getting on the national team even though he had been chosen for the national team's collective training program. "I must make it through the collective training, and I must become a true member of the national team!"

On April 10, 1998, the new iteration of the National Men's Basketball Collective Training team began to assemble in Beijing. In 1998, they had three main missions. The first was to participate in the Friendship Games in New York in July; the second was to compete in the first Asian Professional Basketball League matches to be held from August 14 through September 27 in five different countries and regions; and the third was to defend their crown in the 13th Asian Games in Bangkok, Thailand, at the end of the year.

But as it turned out, Yao Ming was not selected for the 13th Asian Games in Bangkok when the roster of Chinese players was announced on November 6, 1998, by the National Sports Bureau — rather, he was only an "alternate athlete." Those chosen to the team were: Wang Zhizhi, Mengke Bateer, Gong Xiaobin, Liu Yudong, Liu Qiang, Hu Weidong, Sun Jun, Zhang Jinsong, Li Nan, Zhang Wenqi, Li Xiaoyong, and Fan Bin.

This was a bolt from the blue, and it left Yao Ming incomparably dejected.

"At that time, his spirit hit rock bottom, and we did our best to console him - 'don't be too sad, you're still young,'" recalls Yao Ming's teammate Liu Wei.

It is more than cruel for an 18-year-old to fall from the pinnacle of hope into the valley of despair, to encounter great joy and great sorrow at such a young age; however, as far as Yao Ming was concerned, this might have turned out to be a good thing.

In the end, he was able to remain unmoved by either favor or disgrace.

Actually, the main reason why Yao Ming was not chosen for the 13th Asian Games was that the national team was preparing to "use good steel for the edge of the blade." After all, he was only 18 years old, and the Asian Games was nothing more than a "mid-term" for the Asian Championship which was coming up in 1999. The Chinese team's results in the Asian Championship would directly affect whether or not they would be able to participate in the 2000 Olympic Games in Sydney.

Yao Ming was somewhat gratified to be listed along with

Chen Xin'an of the Taipei team as one of the two "best young players" when the Asian Basketball League published its various rankings for Asian men's basketball for the 1998 season on December 4, right before the Bangkok Asian Games began.

"Best all-around player" was Taipei's Zheng Zhilong; "Asia's best center" was Wang Zhizhi; "best point guard" was Zhang Jinsong; and "best small forward" was Japan's Michael Takahashi.

In Bangkok it was a gathering of the greats: all the players on the list of the best in Asian men's basketball went - except for Yao Ming.

What is interesting is that at the Bangkok Asian Games men's basketball arena, the questions most often asked of the Chinese basketball team by the foreign correspondents and scouts were:

"Where is the Chinese team's 7'5" center?"

"Which one of the Chinese players is Yao Ming?"

"Where is Yao Ming?"

The Chinese basketball team replied that Yao Ming was only 18 years old and that the Chinese team was worried that he might get injured playing against adults in the Asian Games, so he wasn't allowed to come to Bangkok.

The scouts were very disappointed not to see Yao Ming in action, and the foreign correspondents immediately asked of the Chinese team:

"Is Yao Ming being saved as a 'secret weapon' for the Asian Championship next year?"

Injuring His Physique

The ball was in mid-air.

Yao Ming and Ouyang Jingui both leaped at the same time, Yao Ming grabbed the ball, and before it left his hands, let forth an earth-shattering moan — Ouyang's foot had stepped heavily on his left instep, instantly fracturing his metatarsal bones.

This was the Shanghai Sharks' final warm-up game before the beginning of the 1998-1999 CBA season, and Ouyang Jingui was the center for the Guangdong Tigers. It was nothing more than an ordinary practice game, nothing more than an ordinary struggle for a rebound, yet the Sharks ended up losing their most important asset.

This was the second time that Yao Ming was injured. The previous injury was at the beginning of 1997, just as he had finally realized the dream of moving up from the youth team to the first national team, and it was also in a minor match: he broke his left ankle bone.

The new season was about to begin, and Yao Ming looked so forlorn with his left foot in a cast.

"Sign your name in commemoration. Maybe it will become a souvenir and fetch a good price," he said jokingly, sticking out his long leg whenever he met somebody.

He had finally gotten a long vacation, but not a vacation he had wished for. The team went out to play, and he stayed in the dormitory by himself, wildly playing computer games and fiercely catching up on all the reading he had never had the time for before. Sometimes he would go to the weight room, and since walking was difficult, he would sit on a bench and work on his upper body.

More and more often he would think about the road he had followed for the past few years, replaying the best and worst games in his mind. If a good friend dropped by to see him, he would latch onto him for a long chat, talking about anything at all, and when the conversation was over, the other person would sigh: Yao Ming is growing more and more mature; his injury has caused his understanding of basketball to increase even more than if he had continued to play!

Although Yao Ming had encountered some twists and turns on the road to the professional basketball, his ability to withstand the physical and mental intimidation of the older players with his frail 17-year-old body, and to become a first-string player on his team during his first season was something not often seen in basketball anywhere in the world.

Yao Ming had garnered all sorts of praise and acclaim, and Yao Ming himself was filled with lofty aspirations; the road ahead had looked smooth — until the fracture arrived.

He had no choice but to lie down, to break away from the never-ending training and matches, from the nitty-gritty technical details, and reexamine himself from another perspective:

What is basketball?

Why do I want to play basketball?

What kind of basketball do I want to play?

An old proverb goes: "A man may lose his horse; yet who can say if this is good or bad?" In other words, what if the horse had disappeared, only to come back later leading another horse? Yao Ming's injury at a key point early on in his career was a fortuitous coincidence, as it gave him the opportunity to calm down and think things over.

As Yao Ming recuperated from his injury and forged his will, thoughts, and aspirations, the Sharks, having lost their inside advantage, found themselves beleaguered by heavy competition.

Beginning with Yao Ming's first season in the CBA, Li Qiuping had designed numerous plays around him which had become better and better with each passing day in competition. But now that Yao Ming was out of the lineup, the Big Shark of Shanghai was missing its sharpest tooth.

This situation was the same as the hardships that Sharks encountered later after Yao Ming left for the NBA — except that later on it was more of a hardship, because the memories that Yao Ming had left behind were very hard for the team to erase.

Yao Ming returned from his injury on February 3, 1999, having missed the first ten regular games of that season.

The opponent that night was the Beijing Aoshen team with Ma Jian, and the Sharks were hosting the competition.

53 minutes into the game, the Sharks had only played 10 minutes of good ball, but that was enough, because that was the 10 minutes that Yao Ming was on the court.

At the end of the first three periods, Shanghai trailed 22 to 26, 37 to 49, and 55 to 70, respectively; during the fourth period they were behind by 10 points, 68 to 78, with only five minutes on the clock.

Li Qiuping called a time-out, and Number 15, Yao Ming, who had not seen a basketball court in quite a while, came in. He was paired up with Zhang Wenqi, Number 6, the team captain, and the two foreign-assistance players, Wei Wen, Number 11, and Ande Lie, Number 10. They were to shut down the visiting team's high scorer, Zhang Tao, Number 10. As expected, this scheme proved effective, and the Sharks surged forward, bringing the score to 82 all. During the final 30 seconds, Zhang Wenqi made three of three free throws, tying the final game score at 85 to 85.

In overtime, the Sharks seized the opportunity in the last two minutes, with both Number 5 Li Jian and Zhang Wenqi hitting three-pointers in succession, and Wei Wen making three for three to widen the score. Shanghai had one the game by five points.

In this match, although Yao Ming scored only 17 points, he did have four rebounds, and he saved the home team at a crucial moment.

The matches followed one after another, and Yao Ming became the nucleus of the team. Gradually, he regained his feel for the basket, stuffing the ball more and more often.

After the conclusion of that season's regulation games, the Sharks were ranked sixth, with 12 wins and 10 losses. But in the post-season playoff games, they were defeated by the Guangdong Tigers.

Judging from appearances, the Sharks did pretty much the same in 1999 season as they had in 1998, and though they even dropped one place in the rankings, Yao Ming knew that now he was different than before.

With no controversy whatsoever he joined the all-star lineup for 1999, and in the North-South All-Star Match in Shanghai on May 8, he was a starter, unlike the previous year in Shenyang where he had spent most of his time on the bench; and he won third place in the slam-dunk competition at half-time.

In the usual recap of the season, although he had missed ten games, he still came in second in dunks, with Wang Zhizhi still ranked first; however, the disparity between them had shrunk from 29 points in 1998 to only 10 in 1999.

What made Yao Ming the proudest was that he was chosen the "most improved player" of the 1998-1999 season.

It was also during this season that the Sharks moved from the Hong Kou Gymnasium to the Hu Wan Gymnasium located in the flourishing downtown area. Afterwards, Yao Ming's family also moved from Shuang Fang Road to a place right across from the Hu Wan Gymnasium, and even though he didn't make it home very often, Yao Zhiyuan and Fang Fengdi found it considerably more convenient to see their son.

From then on, the Hu Wan Gymnasium began to witness the Sharks making history and to witness Yao Ming's transformation from "little big man" to "little giant."

Boys Have Tears

It is very difficult to accurately describe Yao Ming's personality. He is simple and honest, yet also shrewd; he is forthright and yet also persistent. He is very eloquent and has quick reactions, yet sometimes he is overcautious and bashful. Yao Ming himself has stated that he is a multi-faceted person who can speak a common language with people of many levels and many different personalities, but who himself doesn't know what level he belongs to.

Everybody who knows Yao Ming well says that no matter whether it was the green, bashful youth of before or the big-name basketball star of today, in his bones he is still a big kid, and he has a childlike nature that is hard to come by.

He stood out from the crowd even at a young age, and now, even in his 20s, he is carrying great hopes and the heavy pressures that comes with them while living between two extraordinary extremes of public opinion and personal judgment. It is astonishing that he is able to maintain an optimistic and peaceful attitude and retain such a degree of self-control.

This is all attributable to the bright and sunny road of Yao Ming's growth, without entanglements or disappointments or hovering clouds of despair to depress and stifle him. In fact, he had never had unrealistically high hopes. When he was little, his parents never really wanted him to play basketball; they only hoped that he would be a good student like ordinary people and pass the college entrance exams. Later on, when they sent him to the youth sports school to play basketball, they never figured that he would become a famous professional athlete. And after that, when Yao Ming made the youth team through extreme sacrifice and arduous training, their only hope was that he would soon be able to get a good pair of shoes that fit.

At every stage, the goals were limited to that stage. He got to where he is today slowly, gradually, one step at a time, by being down-to-earth, and even more important was that his attitude remained healthy and pure without becoming distorted.

"Yao Ming is very forgiving. He takes the most punishment during a game, and he's so tall; he's tested much, much more than other players the same age, but every time he's fouled, he just laughs it off, and very seldom does he argue with anybody. In a game, if one of the opposing players falls down, he always laboriously bends over to help him up. Then his teammates became dissatisfied: 'When other people knock you down, we don't see them helping you up.' But Yao Ming just dismisses it with a smile. . . ."

Yu Xiaomiao has watched Yao Ming grow from a "hatchling just out of the shell" to a goshawk whose wings flap through the vast heavens, and there is no end to the stories he tells about him.

Fan Bin of the BaYi Rockets is a good friend of Yao Ming's who was his roommate on the national team. Whenever the Rockets and the Sharks have finished a game, if you can't find Yao Ming, just go and look for Fan Bin and you'll find him, and if you want to find Fan Bin, you can call Yao Ming's cell phone, because every time they finish a game, they are sure to have a meal together. But during the first playoff game of the 2000-2001 CBA finals, a rumor started that Yao Ming wanted to fight Fan Bin. What actually happened was that Fan Bin's contact lens got knocked out accidentally by another player, and he was covering his eye, so Yao Ming hurriedly rushed up, asking, "What happened?" But of course the audience couldn't see that, and they thought it was some kind of confrontation.

Yao Ming has always had good relations with others, says Yu Xiaomiao, and this is because of his sincerity toward others: "On the team, it is very normal for the older players to send the younger players to do this or that errand. But Yao Ming never did that, and whenever a dispute arose between the older players and the younger players, he would step forward to calm things down. He always felt that playing for a team meant that you had a responsibility toward the team."

After he joined the youth team in 1994, Yao Ming stayed at the Shanghai Athletics and Sports Technical College at 750 Old Hu Min Road up until the time he went to play in the NBA in October of 2002, and during those eight years, there was not a person at the college who did not like him.

He likes to play video games, which he picks up very rapidly. When he first started, he played simple games like "Solitaire" and "Mine Sweeper," and he got really hooked; sometimes, as soon as practice was over, Yao Ming would turn on his teammate Shen Wei's computer and set new high scores in "Mine Sweeper," leaving Shen Wei, who had a great deal of difficulty making any progress in "Mine Sweeper," stupefied.

Whenever the gang played cards together, Yao Ming would occasionally attempt to steal a good card when he thought someone was not paying attention, though he usually got caught. "Such a big guy dares to steal cards?" they would say. "Don't you know how slow you are?" And then he would chuckle along with everybody.

"Yao Ming is a good guy, he's very affable toward others and extremely polite," says Chef Zhu Yuefang of the "champion mess" at the college's dining hall, who saw that although Yao Ming was the tallest, he wasn't the athlete with the biggest appetite, but he was the most polite athlete.

The class divisions in the dining hall for the provincial-level athletes were very strict, and the top-notch athletes and the ordinary athletes did not eat in the same mess. Yao Ming received special treatment, and even before becoming a top-notch player he began to eat at the "champion mess," where the food standard was high. His favorite was fried chicken wings, and he could eat seven or eight at a meal.

All of the people who ate at the "champion mess" were complex; some of those with accomplishments found it difficult to avoid being cocky, and they would yell bossily at the dining hall workers.

But Yao Ming, with his "Auntie This" and "Auntie That," always spoke so pleasantly, says Zhu Yuefang, a worker in the mess hall. Whenever Yao Ming dined, he would always address her as "Auntie" at least twice, once when he came in and once when he left.

Zhu Yuefang remembers the little things most distinctly, saying, "It is from the little things that one can tell someone's upbringing. Yao Ming is truly good."

As soon as you mention Yao Ming, Shen Peihong, a worker in the college's laundry room, praises him incessantly.

Even though washing one pair of Yao Ming's socks was like washing two pairs of someone else's, Shen Peihong would only charge Yao Ming for one pair.

"He practices so hard, and after practice, you can wring the sweat from the towels," Shen Peihong says.

She came to realize that if somebody who worked so hard didn't win the championship, then who deserved to win it?

On April 10, 2002, in Ningpo, as the first of the championship playoff games between the Sharks and the Rockets began, Shen Peihong was watching television at home. With one minute left in the game, the Sharks led 125 to 124, but because Li Nan of the Rockets made a three-pointer at the very last second, the Rockets stole the first game 127 to 125, and just at the moment that Li Nan made the three-point shot, Shen Peihong had a heart attack and had to be rushed to the hospital for emergency treatment.

That was the first news that Yao Ming heard upon returning to Shanghai.

Unlike most athletes, Yao Ming pays a great deal of attention to major events both at home and abroad. He was the first team member of the Sharks to purchase a notebook computer, which he used both to play games and to surf the internet. If he doesn't go on-line every day to read the news, he will suffer. Before he bought a computer, he liked to read the newspaper. At that time, the newspapers to which the Sharks subscribed were placed in Yu Xiaomiao's room, and Yao Ming became Yu Xiaomiao's frequent visitor.

Yu Xiaomiao uses the term "urbane" to describe Yao Ming. He was born and raised in Shanghai, but he is very adaptable and there is nowhere that he doesn't feel at home, not like a number of Shanghai players, who think that the only good place is Shanghai and complain that it's too cold in Beijing and too hot in Guangzhou.

Yao Ming is truly unlike most Shanghainese in that even today he still has no clear concept of money.

"Whether he's famous or not, Yao Ming never made a fuss about salary and never made any demands of the club," Yu Xiaomiao says.

In the Ninth National Games in 2001, the Sharks lost to the Rockets and took second place. According to the relevant regulations of Shanghai Municipality, the prize for the overall meet champion was 80,000 yuan, ($9,600) and second place was 40,000 yuan ($4,800). However, according to the method of "doubling the total for major sports," the Shanghai Men's Basketball team's silver medal should be 80,000 yuan. The team consisted of 12 members, and the contributions of each were different, so how to distribute the prize money?

The team discussed it for a long time, saying that Yao Ming worked really hard and made a major contribution and should thus get three shares, or 24,000 yuan ($2,900). Then, following repeated deliberation, Yao Ming finally received 14,000 yuan ($1,700) in prize money.

When Yao Ming found out what the amount was, his first reaction was, "You're giving me too much."

"For anyone who is a true professional ballplayer, fame should be a byproduct of basketball," says Yu Xiaomiao. Yao Ming had his own view with regard to money, and he gave an example: "I read a story that told of a young girl who fell in love with an old man, and although the old man's sons and daughters did everything they could to prevent it, the two got married. A few years later, the old man got sick and died, leaving everything to the girl, so his daughters filed a lawsuit, but they lost in court. But then the girl said 'Go ahead, take everything. He is dead; what do I want with it?' What I mean is that love cannot be measured in terms of money, but it can be proved by money; by a similar argument, you can use money to prove other things, like the level of a ballplayer. I haven't been wishing in my heart for money to appear; had it been otherwise, its appearance would have seemed very crass. Of course, I absolutely am not opposed to money, because I need it for my family, and to play games."

Although his impoverished environment as a child left an impression hard to eradicate, Yao Ming's high regard for the spiritual far exceeds the material.

The only time that Yu Xiaomiao ever saw Yao Ming cry was on March 14, 1999. On that day, the Sharks were disgraced in Jinan, suffering a crushing defeat by the Shandong Bulls and losing by 30 points.

The two teams were actually pretty evenly matched, but the Sharks were just not up to par for some reason. First they urgently tried to score points, but they committed one turnover after another. Then, after they had fallen way behind, they got flustered, and offensively they were uncoordinated, attempting wild shots and lowering their scoring percentage, whereas the Shandong Bulls used flexible tactics and remained calm, demolishing the Sharks through an absolutely relentless defense and a multi-faceted offence, 112 to 82.

As soon as the game was over, the Sharks packed up their things, their faces expressionless, and Yao Ming sat to the side, his long legs splayed out. Suddenly, he covered his face and began to bawl.

Wang Zhongguang, then coach of the Sharks, asked, "Yao Ming, what are you crying for?"

Yao Ming sobbed, "How could we lose so bad? . . ."

He was growing up.

Asian Championship

On May 19, 1999, the National Sports Bureau's Basketball Administration Center formally announced that in order to prepare for the 20th Asian Men's Basketball Championship and the preliminary qualifying games for the 2000 Olympics Games, the Chinese National Men's Basketball Group Training team would begin group training at once.

There were 15 players on the overall roster: Mengke Bateer (Beijing), Li Xiaoyong (Liaoning), Sun Jun (Ji Lin), Yao Ming and Zhang Wenqi (Shanghai), Hu Weidong and Zhang Cheng (Jiangsu), Gong Xiaobin and Cheng Zhiming (Shandong), Li Qun (Guangdong), and Wang Zhizhi, Liu Yudong, Zhang Jinsong,

Li Nan, and Fan Bin (BaYi).

Jiang Xingquan served as the head coach of the new National Men's Basketball team, Li Jinsheng, chairman of the Basketball Administration Center, served as team leader, and Min Lulei served as assistant coach. Jiang Xingquan was the most successful coach in the history of Chinese men's basketball. In 1994, he was the head coach who led the Chinese Men's Basketball team to win eighth place in the World Championship, the best that Chinese men's basketball had ever achieved. In May 1995, he was transferred to serve as vice-chairman of the Liaoning Provincial Sports Commission, and in May 1999, when he won the "award for outstanding contributions in new Chinese basketball" bestowed by the Chinese Basketball Association and again assumed the important mission of head-coaching the Chinese Men's Basketball team, he was leading a comfortable and carefree life as head of the Liaoning Provincial Athletics and Sports Academy.

There was only one way for Chinese men's basketball: they must win the crown at the Asian Championship held in Fukuoka, Japan, thus obtaining the only Asian ticket into the 2000 Olympics at Sydney — the Chinese women's team only got third place in the Asian Championship and was thus not included in the playoff pool for selection to the Olympics. The men's team had not been able to participate in the preceding World Championships, and the Chinese teams had come home in defeat from the World Youth Championships and the World Collegiate Championships. So now their backs were to the wall, and they simply had no choice but to win.

Beginning in May, 1999, the National Men's Basketball Group Training team commenced its group training program on the shores of Lake Kalun in the northern city of Changchun. For over 30 days, sweat fell like rain, and Yao Ming was one of the ones who sweated the most. His qualifications were good but his seniority was low, and he had no choice but to train hard.

On June 13, after the close of group training, the Chinese Men's Basketball team took part in the first Asian Professional Basketball Superleague match. As the pre-match warm-ups began, Jiang Xingquan's goal was obvious: to try out the lineup.

The opponent in the first match was the Japan All-Stars, a team without any national team players, and in the first and second halves of the game, the Chinese Men's Basketball team tried out two different lineups and types of play, easily winning 93 to 71.

Yao Ming was part of the second lineup. The Chinese team's starting lineup consisted of center Wang Zhizhi, forwards Gong Xiaobin and Sun Jun, and guards Li Xiaoyong and Zhang Jinsong. The Chinese team, which had been in group training for the last month, had some difficulty at the beginning of the game in adapting to their opponent's press defense and fast-break offense, and after two minutes they were down to the Japanese team 6 to 4. After Jiang Xingquan called a time-out, the Chinese team went on a 14-to-2 run and turned the game into a fast-break and three-point show, leading 50 to 32 at the end of the first half.

In the second half, Jiang Xingquan sent out the other new lineup: the center was Yao Ming, the forwards were Mengke Bateer and Hu Weidong, and the guards were Li Nan and Fan Bin. Yao Ming's long arms immediately put a "canopy" over the Japanese team to reject the opposition's shots three times in succession, enabling the Chinese team to take a 73-52 lead in the third quarter and emerge with a 22-point victory over their opponents, 93 to 71.

After the game, Jiang Xing Quan said, "We regarded this match as part of our training, so in the morning we conducted a two-hour fast-paced stamina training session, and some of the players got cramps due to the hot weather. Today we mainly practiced offense-defense tempo transitions. We didn't play any games after the league matches were over, and so in our first outing today we committed 22 turnovers. The other team played at a fast pace, and no matter how far we were ahead, they never gave up, giving us good practice in offense-defense transition, footwork, and defensive ability."

This was Yao Ming's first game under Jiang Xingquan's command.

Subsequently, the Chinese Men's Basketball team played a number of games in swift succession, winning them all easily. There is no doubt that Yao Ming, not yet 19 years old, made a deep impression on Jiang Xingquan.

In the game with the Hong Kong Wei Li Team in Shenzhen on June14, Yao Ming went on in the second half with Mengke Bateer, Hu Weidong, Li Nan, and Fan Bin. He immediately shut down the Hong Kong Wei Li Team's center, and before the third quarter was over, Yao Ming took a long pass from Fan Bin on the run, made a 180-degree turn, and launched a hook shot with his back to the basket, sending the arena into a frenzy. On June 18, the team went to Hong Kong where they played against the Korean All-Star team, and although the Chinese Men's Basketball team won, their performance was just ordinary; however, Yao Ming, who played half the game, was high scorer for the Chinese team with 16 points.

On June 19, after the two matches at Guangdong and Hong Kong, Jiang Xingquan summed up the performance of the newly organized national team thusly: "What stuck out the most was that the style of the whole team on the court was still not too stiff, and next, they still need to strengthen their defense, rebounding, and running." He said that through these two matches he now knew what to do with the Chinese team's main lineup.

Yao Ming himself also knew what to do. He was no longer worried so much about wins and losses as he had been when first selected to the national group training team, and the more games he played, the better he came to understand his own strengths.

On August 28, Yao Ming stood in the gymnasium in Fukuoka, Japan, with the characters Zhong Guo (China) on the front of his jersey.

This time was different from the disappointment of 1998, when he hadn't been selected for the Asian Games in Bangkok. Now, of the 15 members of the group training team, there were three who hadn't been chosen — Zhang Cheng (Jiangsu), Cheng Zhiming (Shandong), and Li Qun (Guangdong).

In fact, Yao Ming, who was just half a month shy of his 19th birthday on this hot summer day in 1999, had become one of the 12 best players in Chinese men's basketball.

The Chinese team's first opponent in the Asian Championship was Malaysia, and everybody felt that this would be a lopsided match; but the results surprised everybody — due to the tenacious attack of the Malaysian team, the Chinese team was able to win — but only by a score of 54 to 41.

The Chinese team was apparently not up to speed. Although

they were big and tall and had lots of experience, they were only playing at fifty to sixty percent in terms of shooting percentage, rebounds, and formations. Although the Malaysian players were relatively short by comparison, they were agile runners and their shooting percentage was high, so much so that at time it looked as though they were stringing the Chinese team along. The 6'0" point guard Tang Jixian, "small in stature but big in spirit," directly confronted all the big, tall Chinese players, and dared to run right through them and dunk. This move of his resulted in the most beautiful basket of the game, winning the applause of the whole house.

In contrast, although the Chinese team towered above their opponents, they could not match them in agility or speed. Though the Chinese team was never behind in the entire game, they were closely pursued by their opponent throughout and were able to maintain the lead only with difficulty. Jiang Xingquan said, "Their goal was not to lose big, so when they got the ball, they ran out the clock, and we ended up looking flustered and agitated." But Malaysia's head coach Felton Sealey sneered, "The Chinese team did not play up to the level they should have; they were all asleep."

But when it came to Yao Ming, Sealey was at a loss. Jiang Xingquan had kept his main center Wang Zhizhi on ice for the first half, substituting center Yao Ming and giving him free rein, and the opponents could do nothing in the face of his shot-blocking, while he also became the game's top scorer at 19 points. Liu Yudong scored 10 points, the only other Chinese player to break into double digits.

On August 29, the Chinese team took on Syria, the West Asian champion, and shaking off their slump of the previous day, won a huge victory, 112 to 61.

Jiang Xingquan was very confident, for as soon as the game began, the Chinese team attacked fiercely in wave after wave, leading 17 to 2 before the five-minute mark, and in the first ten minutes or so, the Chinese team's lead reached 38 to 2. Moreover, the Chinese team's defense was also very tight, and in the first twelve minutes of the game they did not allow their opponents to score a single opposing basket, as the four points the Syrian team scored during this time were all free-throws. In the second half, Jiang Xingquan rotated all twelve players into the lineup and tried out the "dual-center" tactic with Wang Zhizhi and Yao Ming, which allowed the Syrian team to catch up just a bit.

In this game, Yao Ming revealed another trick, not his "Yao Ming canopy" but rather his most proper English — although it was only two words. He was struggling for the ball with Osama Madani of the Syrian team, in his own half of the court, and in the confusion the ball went out of bounds at the baseline. The referee gave the ball to the Syrian team, and Yao Ming, with a pained expression on his face, immediately asked the referee, "Mine?" Then he pointed to Madani and said, "He!"

The referee paid him no attention and gave possession to the Syrian team.

Even so, his team was filled with deep admiration.

Yao Ming's sincerity and good-heartedness, just like his hard work and sacrifice, made a deep impression on his fellow players on the national team, and the more time they spent together, the more everyone realized how interesting and likeable this guy from Shanghai was.

As far as the opponents were concerned, Yao Ming was becoming more and more "fearsome," far exceeding the high level of opposition in the CBA league matches, like some tremendous external force whose alarming potential had been summoned to life and was now exploding.

The Chinese team's third match was a great 91-to-54 victory over the Kuwait team, and Yao Ming was the star of the game; although his point total of 20 was three less than that of his teammate Wang Zhizhi, he was the player with the most positive and enthusiastic play.

He only played for the first half, but his shooting percentage was 100%, making 9 out of 9 field goals and two out of two free throws; he also got six rebounds, dunked five times, and blocked three shots, and did not have a single turnover.

This was Yao Ming's finest performance since joining the national team.

The Asian Championship was the key period during which Yao Ming displayed his true ability and gained confidence. He was no longer that clumsy young man who had suffered 15 knockdowns in one game, and he was no longer the wide-eyed, hapless substitute center, the "Shanghai Wang Zhizhi." In fact, in the statistics for the six games of the Chinese team in the Asian Championship published on September 4 before the final game, Yao Ming was first in several categories: he had the most rebounds, at 40; he had blocked the most shots, 17; and his shooting percentage was the highest, making 28 of 35.

He also displayed his awesome offensive ability. Nobody could handle him inside, and he had scored 74 points in the six games, second only to Wang Zhizhi's 80 points.

Also, he ranked fourth among the 12 national team players in terms of time on the court — Yao Ming was no longer the rookie sent into the game for practice when the national team was way ahead.

"When Yao Ming first came to the national team's group training camp, he was far inferior in opposing other centers, but now he has displayed very visible improvement." This was Jiang Xingquan's critique of Yao Ming following the Asian Championship.

On September 5, 1999, the Chinese Men's Basketball team struck down the Korean team, the defending champions, 63 to 45, again ascending the championship throne in the Asian Men's Basketball Championship. This was Yao Ming's first Asian championship.

A tide of emotion surged through Yao Ming as he stood on the podium and watched the Chinese national flag being hoisted during the awards ceremony.

He had been playing professional league matches for less than two years, and already he had become one of Asia's first-ranked players.

6.   So Near Yet So Far

Events of the Past

The National Basketball Association is full of stories. The on and off-court dramas of the young, talented, wealthy, and good-looking players attract the attention of the entire world.

In this world there were virtually no Chinese. The first Chinese to sign an NBA contract was Song Tao.

Song Tao, born in 1964, was a 6'7" center from Shandong. In the 1986 World Men's Basketball Championship, the Chinese team came in ninth, which was the best achievement at that time for Chinese basketball in major world-class matches, and Song Tao put on a distinguished showing for the Chinese team.

And it was in this World Championship that the young Song Tao came to the attention of the world.

Just like Yao Ming today, Song Tao was regarded by his generation of basketball experts as China's basketball hope. People remember Song Tao for his springiness and excellent physique. In the national slam-dunk competition he could dunk by holding the ball in both hands at once, and his ability to hang in midair was remarkable. Because of his explosiveness and springiness, the coach of the national track and field team had tried to talk Song Tao into changing careers, joking that "If Song Tao practices high-jumping, then Zhu Jianhua (who was then the leading high-jumper) will be out of a job!"

As a center, Song Tao was the type of agile player with a large range of movement and a good grasp of skills and strategy. His dunking form was extraordinarily beautiful, and his shot-blocking ability was also first-rate; he could regularly block opponents even when separated by another player, and in a match when visiting America, he even blocked superstar Julius Erving.

In June 1987, Song Tao came to America and signed a contract with the Atlanta Hawks, who selected him in the 3rd round of the NBA draft. But fate is so mysterious: he then suffered a series of injuries and illnesses, and in the end Song Tao never was able to become the first Chinese to play in the NBA.

In 1985, in the last practice session before the Chinese Men's Basketball team left to compete in the World College Sports Meet, Song Tao successfully halted his opponent's attack with a beautiful block, but at the same time he fell heavily to the floor, and the knee which hit the floor first was instantly shattered into more than ten fragments.

Even so, the Atlanta Hawks were still thirsting for Song Tao, because the star Arvydas Sabonis, who incurred an injury similar to that of Song Tao around the same time, was able to successfully return to the court following surgical treatment. The American doctor who gave Sabonis a second lease on life also operated successfully on Song Tao, and after 100 days he was able to resume physical training.

While Song Tao had recovered to the point where he could run a quarter mile, one day he carelessly stepped in some water in the bathroom and slipped, fracturing his knee again. The second knee injury ended his trip to the NBA

The Atlanta Hawks, infatuated with Song Tao, kept his

uniform for a long time afterwards, but they were never able to consummate the deal. Sabonis was running around like before, but all Song Tao could do was to give a deep sigh and return to obscurity.

In the end, Song Tao retired from the national team and settled down in Taiwan, and now he travels back and forth between Taiwan and China, still engaged in the business of basketball.

The next protagonist to come onto the court was Ma Jian.

Ma Jian, a native of Hebei Province, was born in 1969 and was 6'7". In 1986 he joined the youth team, and in 1998 he joined the national team. In 1992 he had gone on his own to study abroad in America, and from 1993 to 1994 he was the first Chinese in the NCAA (the American collegiate basketball league).

However, Ma Jian was unable to advance any further. In 1995 and 1996 he participated in the training camp of the Los Angeles Lakers with the intention of taking part in the NBA draft. At the time he was full of confidence and it didn't occur to him that he might not be chosen. In the final round Ma Jian fell one step short: he became the Lakers' 13th player. Ma Jian later remembered, "When I wasn't picked, I felt very regretful, very sad, and very sorry. But afterwards, I felt that I was very successful, very proud, and very replenished; after all, I was the first Chinese to come so close to the NBA."

In 1998, Ma Jian returned to China to join the CBA, but then became mired in a lawsuit. Now he serves the Shanghai Sharks following the departure of Yao Ming, sitting patiently on the bench and waiting for his knee injury to recover.

Next comes the story of Hu Weidong.

On March 17, 2000, the Chinese Basketball Association received a fax from General Manager John Gabriel of the Orlando Magic inviting Hu Weidong, star player of the Jiangsu Dragons, to join the Orlando Magic, and there was also an accompanying detailed contract, which stipulated the hope that Hu would be able to take part in NBA regulation games from March 21 through March 31 on behalf of the Orlando Magic.

Gabriel clearly specified in the contract document that Hu Weidong would assist the Orlando Magic from March 21 through March 31, and also proffered relatively substantial payment — Hu Weidong's compensation for ten days of play with the Orlando Magic would be US$17,757, with a per diem allowance of US$88 for expenses. Hu Weidong's lodging was already arranged.

The Chinese Basketball Association responded with the statement: "As long as preparations of the Chinese Men's Basketball team for the Sydney Olympics are not affected, the Chinese Basketball Association supports this."

Whenever a major player on an NBA team is injured, that team will consider signing a short-term contract with a player outside the NBA to act as a replacement and to help the team. The Orlando Magic were currently ranked eighth in the Eastern Conference and had hopes of making the post-season playoffs, but at a key time their offensive guard Chauncey Billups and forward Jeff Halpern were both injured, and the guard position was relying solely on the Herculean efforts of Ron Mercer; thus Hu Weidong, who had just been crowned "long-shot king," "scoring king" and "steals king" for the 1999-2000 CBA season, and who was the Chinese player with the most well-rounded skills, became the natural choice to meet their needs.

However, Hu Weidong ultimately refused this short-term offer for numerous reasons: his leg injury had not yet fully healed, there were "too few games and he would not be able to display his full worth," it was too short notice and the procedures were difficult to arrange, and it would affect his preparations for the Olympics.

On June 10, 1997, a dispatch sent by Xinhua News Agency reporter Xu Jicheng from Salt Lake City, featuring an interview with NBA Commissioner David Stern, drew a huge reaction.

"In the not-too-distant future, China will become the world's largest basketball market," Stern had said. Stern had been NBA Commissioner since 1984, and during his thirteen-year tenure, the NBA's annual revenue had risen from an initial figure of US$190 million to US$4 billion by 1997, surpassing such professional sports as football, baseball, and hockey to become the largest professional sports organization in America.

At that time, Yao Ming was about to make his stunning emergence in adult matches, Mengke Bateer was marshaling his strength in silent competition, and Wang Zhizhi, who had had a successful career as a youth, had already attracted the attention of the NBA.

This abundant flow of talented Chinese basketball players was to meld into world basketball competition at the highest level. Led in earlier years by the isolated struggles of Song Tao and Ma Jian, it was about to become a rushing torrent.

Eighth Wonder

In July 1998, when journalist Robin Miller first saw Yao Ming, his excitement, enthusiasm and astonishment were fully revealed in an article he wrote for the Indianapolis Star:

"His name is Yao Ming, and on the basketball court he is the eighth wonder of the world. He's 7 feet 5 inches tall, weighs 252 pounds, has an arm span of 9 feet 3 inches, and can make 15-foot jump shots with agility; he can also turn and attack beneath the basket. He's only 17 years old, one of the many good, tall players at the Nike Basketball Training Camp here, but compared with these other young basketball players he stands out like a crane among chickens. . . ."

For an American paper to use "eighth wonder" to describe a young basketball player seems quite without precedent.

On June 14, 1998, Yao Ming and Liu Wei, his teammate on the Shanghai Sharks, together with Head Coach Li Qiuping and the club's General Manager Li Yaomin traveled as a group to America to take part in the Nike summer camp for young basketball players.

The first stop on their journey was the basketball camp in San Diego, California. The city of San Diego was just recovering from a large fire which had burned nearby, and the basketball gym was still filled with the smell of thick smoke; but Yao Ming and Liu Wei didn't notice it — they were too excited.

Here Yao Ming and Liu Wei underwent a two-week period of training, and received tips from scouting coach Tates Locke of the Portland Trailblazers. The 1997 NBA draft notable Tyson Chandler also trained there at the same time as Yao Ming and Liu Wei.

Yao Ming remembers, "This guy has a great body, and it's like he has springs in his feet — he goes straight up and down, but I'm a lot taller than he is, so we had a lot of laughs while training together. One time we were doing center sliding-step training, with two people facing each other and sliding three steps to the side while jumping up and slapping hands, six repetitions in all. The coach said that whoever didn't make a loud sound when slapping hands would have to run laps as punishment. When our group's turn came, we did it once and the coach told us to stop, but he didn't make us run laps. He was so happy he could hardly catch his breath, and our teammates all around us were all happily sitting on the floor. When we jumped up simultaneously, Chandler could only come up to my elbow, so there was no way that we could slap hands."

Tyson Chandler, who had encountered a "tall man," was surrounded by laughter; he vigorously rubbed the back of his head, as though he couldn't figure out what was going on. The next day, the local newspaper published an article in the sports section: "Look, It's the Elbow-Slapping Exercise!"

Their itinerary was very tight, and then they went to Indianapolis, where they stayed for a full ten days and participated in some Upper Midwest League matches. Then they finally arrived at the Michael Jordan training camp. After those happy but all too fleeting days had passed, Yao Ming was also invited to participate in a five-day summer camp for big men in Hawaii, but what about the other three? After talking it over, they decided to go home.

The trip to America lasted less than two months, and Yao Ming took part in nearly 30 games, more than the number of games that the youth team back home would play in two years.

U.S. basketball made an unforgettable impression on Yao Ming, and both he and Liu Wei learned a lot with regard to techniques for increasing their resistance, successful rebounding, and shooting.

"Those days were pretty arduous, and my deepest impression is that I couldn't get enough to eat. Our expenses were limited, and there were three days when we ate lunch and dinner combined. I got injured and didn't have to play, so I had a hamburger, but Yao Ming still had to play, and all he had to eat was two hamburgers. By the time we got back home to Shanghai, he had grown a bit thinner, but he was still very excited," Liu Wei remembers.

Of the 40 best prospects for center from all over America at the Jordan training camp, Yao Ming ranked second. His American coach Bob Watson said, "When I saw him last year, he was 7 feet 3 inches, and this year he has grown to 7 feet 5 inches. He is an agile giant. His two legs have developed strength, but he still needs to strengthen his upper body and improve his running technique. But he's only been competing for two and a half years. Last year I saw him at the training camp in Paris, and this year he has already progressed by leaps and bounds. He is going to become an extraordinarily outstanding player, and he himself wants to continuously improve."

What Watson was referring to was the European basketball training camp held in Paris in the summer of 1997. It was Yao Ming's first trip abroad. The European basketball training camp brought together the world's top coaches and the most promising young basketball players from all countries. China's representatives were Yao Ming, Jin Lipeng and Chen Ke.

Even though the training camp lasted only about two weeks

or less, it was very meaningful to Yao Ming to be among people of the same age from countries all over the world, and it was a major boost to his confidence; although he didn't play in any adult matches, he had already confirmed his goal: "I want to become China's best center."

At the 1998 Jordan camp, Yao Ming, who had already had a year of CBA experience, when surrounded by NBA scouts, came to understand even more deeply that his "future was not just a dream."

Scouts from various NBA teams regularly gather at the Jordan summer camp as well as other training camps across the country. They fully honored the NBA's written regulations and avoided all direct contact with the players, but they had already begun to look very closely at Yao Ming.

The basketball coaches from the various NBA teams were the same, but they were in a more favorable position and could have personal contact with Yao Ming — and Yao Ming began to encounter the greatest temptations of his 17 years.

First was Assistant Coach Glenn Wilkes of the Orlando Magic, who after seeing Yao Ming practice, immediately told Li Yaomin, "Yao Ming is ready to play in the NBA!" Then there was Tates Locke of the Portland Trailblazers, who, after personally leading a training session for Yao Ming, made a proposal to Li Yaomin about transferring Yao Ming and offered a trade fee of US$1,000,000. John Thomson of the Washington Wizards cornered Li Yaomin on the spot: "We can sign a contract now for Yao Ming with a trade fee of a million a year, for three years!" The person in charge of the Wizards' finances made a special trip to go see Yao Ming and agreed to a trade fee of 1 million on the spot, saying that if Yao Ming couldn't show up right away he could send Thomson on a special trip to Shanghai to train Yao Ming for a month or two.

Yao Ming was already used to causing a stir wherever he went. On May 12, 1997, before he had ever played in any adult games, Yao Ming went with a group to visit Taiwan, becoming a traveling exhibition on the island. At a press conference held by the Taiwan basketball association, a local reporter asked him, "Can you stay in Taiwan to play? We can invite an American coach to conduct your training."

At the time, Yao Ming's voice was still raspy and adolescent: "I am a Shanghainese and I want to play for Shanghai. I can get very good training in Shanghai."

During the flight home to Shanghai, team leader Yu Xiaomiao realized that Yao Ming had disappeared. When they arrived at Hong Qiao Airport in Shanghai, Yao Ming came running out of the front of the plane, saying that the captain had invited him to go to the cockpit.

To play in the NBA is the ultimate dream of every basketball player, and Yao Ming was no exception. Now, with the dream right in front of him, close enough to reach out and touch, Yao Ming heard clearly all the persuasive talk of the NBA representative: if he were willing to go right now, he wouldn't even have to participate in the draft!

Yao Ming himself felt that the thing to do was to "first play well at home; if I couldn't even play well at home, then what would be the use of going to the NBA?"

Yao Ming won't forget his first trip to America. Of course, it was at the summer camp that he had the good fortune to match skills with Jordan himself on the same court, and a couple of Yao Ming's three-pointers left a deep impression on Jordan.

Later on, a lot of people asked Yao Ming: "Did you block any of Jordan's shots?"

Yao Ming would always laugh, "That would never do; no matter what, you had to give Jordan a little face!"

Three Years of Hardship

On May 5, 1999, the *Washington Post* published a report that really stirred up the Americans: "Yao Ming, the 18-year-old Chinese little giant, has reached an agreement with Evergreen Sports, a Cleveland, Ohio management company, and is preparing to participate in the NBA rookie draft next month."

The *Washington Post* said, "This center for the Shanghai Sharks affiliated with the Chinese Basketball Association is an outstanding young prospect discovered by scouts overseas. His manager feels that Yao Ming will be chosen in the first round of the draft and has an unlimited future." The report quoted the words of Evergreen president Michael Coyne: "Judging from Yao Ming's height and mobility as well as his intelligence and obedience, we believe that he will be the first pick in this year's NBA draft."

But on the very same day, Fang Fengdi and Yao Zhiyuan issued a statement to the effect that Yao Ming would not participate in the draft and broke off the management agreement with Evergreen. The Yao family's reasons were: Although Yao Ming was now 7'3", he was still young, and not strong enough; if he entered the NBA it would be hard for him to stand up to the opponents, so they were prepared to wait and consider other opportunities later on.

At the 1998-1999 season CBA All-Star Game on May 8, Li Yaomin, assistant general manager of the Shanghai Sharks, confirmed the news for a Xinhua News Agency reporter that Yao Ming would not take part in the NBA draft.

Li Yaomin's explanation was that on May 1 Yao Ming and Evergreen had jointly signed a document stipulating that the said company would represent Yao Ming in participation in the NBA draft in June 1999 as well as in other related matters, "but after several days of considering many aspects, Yao Ming's family issued a statement on May 5 breaking off the management agreement with Evergreen."

The management agreement between Yao Ming and Evergreen was for three years, and in accordance with the requirements of the Shanghai Municipal Sports Bureau, Yao Ming was to first take part in the draft and then go to play in the NBA after playing in the Ninth National Games in 2001. During this period, Evergreen Sports was to have been responsible for organizing training in America to give Yao Ming skills training and body-ability training. In addition, the agreement also stipulated that Evergreen Sports would also select other young members of the Shanghai Sharks each year and send them to America for group training, make arrangements for American trainers to view video tape recordings of the Sharks' matches, assist in providing opinions regarding progress and improvement, assist and fund the introduction of foreign assistance for the team to fill the gap left by Yao Ming's departure, assist the team in broadening its marketing and development, etc., and because of these advance additions, once Yao Ming had been drafted and signed a contract, Evergreen Sports, in addition to obtaining the agreed-upon contract representation fee stipulated by NBA regulations, would also take one third of Yao Ming's profits after he joined the NBA.

Perhaps it was because this number was too large that the Yao family felt the arrangement "unreasonable" and refused to let Yao Ming proceed — but the written agreement, in black and white, was already legally in effect, and because of this agreement, Yao Ming suffered three years of hardship. In 2001, when outsiders all felt the time was ripe, Yao Ming still did not participate in the draft, and no one can say that it was not due to the effect of this agreement. Had Yao Ming taken part in the draft at that time, Evergreen Sports could have filed a lawsuit, and what everyone feared most was Yao Ming getting tangled up in some legal action before he had even gone to America.

It wasn't until four years later, on June 22, 2002, that Yao Ming's representative, after finally concluding an agreement with the Shanghai Sharks to allow Yao Ming to play in America, held an "Information Meeting on Yao Ming's Going to America" at the Regal Hotel in Shanghai, at which Wang Xiaopeng, a lawyer retained by Yao Ming, said of the agreement with Evergreen Sports:

"As far as the Evergreen contract is concerned, Bai Li, the general manager of the Sharks, has indicated to us that he is not in agreement with it. The Evergreen contract was signed with Yao Ming and has nothing to do with us. I don't think that this contract has affected us in representing Yao Ming. The NBA Players' Union also feels that the Evergreen contract severely impinges upon the interests of the player and is legally untenable. This contract has implications with regard to both Chinese and American law, and we also hold our own views regarding it; we have even hired an American lawyer to analyze the contract. We feel that this contract is severely detrimental to Yao Ming's interests, which was already known, and therefore it is inappropriate to discuss this contract again at the present time. This problem no longer poses any obstacle to Yao Ming."

The signing of this unreasonable contract was not, as general opinion portrayed it at the time, a "surprise attack" or "rash and careless"; rather, both sides carried out a serious study of the concrete details of the agreement before signing.

The only thing is that in those days, even the Shanghainese, who are strongly aware of the importance of contracts, didn't have that good an understanding of the NBA and especially the NBA's laws, and there was a certain amount of impetuosity — who wouldn't want to become the first Chinese to go to the NBA?

On March 30, 2000, when NBA Commissioner Stern first revealed his inner thoughts regarding Chinese basketball, he said that Chinese players wanting to play in the NBA shouldn't be too hasty; only if they went one step at a time would they be able to succeed.

At that time, at the St. Regis Hotel in Beijing, Stern used advanced synchronized audio-visual equipment to carry out a teleconference with Beijing's basketball reporters. In responding to a question about how Asian players could play for the NBA, he said, "The NBA was able to develop to its current state through more than half a century of tempering; and if Chinese and other Asian players want to get into the NBA, the levels of local basketball must be raised, and they must not be impatient."

Yao Ming calmly accepted that he could not be in the draft in 1999; in hosting a news conference, he himself indicated that "at present I am still comparatively young, and let's wait and see whether I can go to the NBA later. The leadership of the club and the municipal sports committee took part in and guided the entire process of discussions and contract signing this time, and therefore the explanation of the club and sports committee leadership is ultimately the accurate one."

Although he was unable to go to the NBA for the time being, the NBA nevertheless still remembered Yao Ming, and before the 2000 Olympics in Sydney, Bruce O'Neil, head of the American Basketball Academy, provided the money for Yao Ming to make another trip to train in America.

Later, Yao Ming told a story about "The Need for Speed":

"In 2000, my skills were still pretty rough, and sometimes I would even blush with embarrassment. But as soon as Bruce O'Neil saw me, it was like I was his darling, and he came up and gave me a big hug. But instead of being hugged by my arms, I should say he got hugged by my ribs.

"Then we worked out and played some games, and he kept his eyes on me the whole time. And then he got somebody to tell me that he had a very good friend called Charlie Brown, who was the coach of Shaquille O'Neal, and if he were allowed to train me for two years, he guaranteed that I would be more agile than Hakeem Olajuwon, fiercer than Patrick Ewing, and a better shooter than David Robinson! I was dumbfounded. Could this old guy be telling the truth? I thought it over, and though I wasn't sure about the other stuff, I knew for certain that I would be better looking than Ewing.

"I have to say that Bruce O'Neil was really good to me. When he saw me standing next to his own car, he immediately gave me the keys and let me drive it around for fun. He was my co-driver. The westerners in America are very down-to-earth and yet very idealistic, so some of the easterners say that the westerners are all "farmers." Old Bruce was the head of an academy, but he was always happy to see you, more like the school janitor or handyman.

"So if Uncle Bruce said drive, then we would drive. I had the translator sit in the back seat, and he was telling me what Uncle Bruce was saying. To tell the truth, I drove pretty fast, and Uncle Bruce told me how good I was driving. So after we finished taking a spin, he insisted that I must be a 'professional' driver. Right away I told the translator to tell him that I was truly a 'rookie' and didn't even have a driver's license.

"As soon as he heard this, his jaw dropped in fright, and he immediately asked, 'Then how come you dare to drive so fast?'

"So all I could do was be truthful: 'As soon as I started to drive, it seemed like I was playing the game *The Need for Speed*, and if I crashed, then I would still have two lives left, so I just went for it.'

"After the old man finished listening to me, he mumbled something and got out of the car, and then I asked the translator what he had said.

"The translator laughed and told me: the old man said that for sure you will do OK!"

Three Suitable Conditions

"Yao Ming will not participate in the 2001 NBA draft."

On the afternoon of May 11, 2001, in the Shanghai Sharks' conference room, surrounded by cameras, microphones, and hopeful stares, Club General Manager Bai Li made the formal announcement.

All the reporters were speechless. Bai Li emphasized, "Our decision was reached after repeated contact and discussion with the Basketball Management Center, the Shanghai Municipal Sports Bureau, Yao Ming's parents, and Yao Ming himself."

The briefing was originally scheduled to start at 3:30 in the afternoon, but Bai Li, Assistant General Manager Li Yaomin, and Yao Ming's parents were late, and the crush of reporters waited for 15 minutes. Then Li Yaomin provided an explanation: "Why did we delay until 3:45 to start the meeting? Because at 3:30 we were still carrying out the last bit of discussions with the Basketball Management Center, the Shanghai Municipal Sports Bureau, and other concerned parties."

Bai Li listed five main reasons for Yao Ming's not participating in the 2001 draft:

(1) Chinese basketball, and especially the CBA, which was just in its startup stage, needed star players like Yao Ming for overall support;

(2) The mission of the national team in competition this year was a heavy one, including the East Asian Games, the Asian Championship, and the World Collegiate Sports Meet, and if Yao Ming were to go to the NBA, it would certainly affect his practice with the national team;

(3) The people of Shanghai needed Yao Ming to participate in the Ninth National Games to win glory for Shanghai and for the club;

(4) The NBA required that young players before their 22nd birthday must participate in the NBA draft of their own volition and thus must be fully prepared physically and mentally before going to the NBA, whereas the club felt that at present Yao Ming was somewhat lacking in this respect; and

(5) Yao Ming should join the NBA as a world-class basketball star symbolically representing the Chinese people, and there was no need to be impatient or agitated about it.

Earlier, when visited by representatives from American cable network HBO Sports, Bei Genyuan, chairman of the Sharks, had indicated that Yao Ming's entry into the NBA must adhere to three principles: "The right time, the right team, and the right conditions for cooperation."

There was no doubting the imminent approach of the Ninth National Games, and therefore it was not "the right time" for Yao Ming to join the NBA.

Bai Li said, "The Shanghai team is very willing to allow Yao Ming to go to the NBA to develop further. However, we all know that this year is the year of the Ninth National, and Yao Ming was nurtured by Shanghai single-handedly, so of course Shanghai hopes that Yao Ming can contribute." Li Yaomin elaborated, "If Yao Ming participates in the draft, he will get a position extremely toward the front. In that case, it goes without saying that the team that picks Yao Ming will have high hopes for him. But if Yao Ming is to represent Shanghai to play in the Ninth National Games, then there is no way that he could participate in either the NBA training camp in August of this year or the warm-up games in October. So according to NBA rules, he would not be able to represent his team by competing in regulation games. This is not good for Yao Ming, and it might have a big impact on his value as a player."

Only forty days earlier, Wang Zhizhi had joined the Dallas Mavericks.

At that moment, Yao Ming was far away in Beijing taking part in group training for the National team, and Fang Fengdi, who had attended the briefing on his behalf, was very calm, but those who looked closely could see this mother's regret.

In speaking of her own son, she candidly revealed: "Yao Ming's success today is inseparable from the concern and support of the leadership at various levels, the coaches, the media, and the fans. Everyone has put a lot of effort into him, and as his mother, I want to express my heartfelt gratitude to everyone, and I hope that in the future everyone will continue to be concerned for Yao Ming. Yao Ming is a sincere child, and these past few years he has been exhausted both physically and emotionally, so if he says something inappropriate, I ask everyone to please forgive him."

As she spoke, Fang Fengdi could not conceal how proud she was of her son, how much she cherished him, and how high were her expectations for him. "To play in the NBA is every basketball player's dream. I was also an athlete, and I have also had this kind of experience. Now Yao Ming has this dream, and I am very happy. A person must have a dream in order to be motivated, to progress, and now we have to take this overall goal and break it down into smaller steps in order to achieve it...I hope Yao Ming's dream comes true."

After the briefing was over and Fang Fengdi was being interviewed by the press, she had this to say concerning what Bai Li had said about Yao Ming's not being ready: "The club's 'not being ready' doesn't refer to level of skill or physical condition, because in those areas Yao Ming ought not to have any problems. What the club was referring to when it said 'not being ready' was mostly the mental or emotional aspect. Yao Ming is still too soft, his personality lacks that certain tiger-like ferocity, and his will is not sufficient; he is easily satisfied, but I'm sure he will make progress in the big games coming up."

During the 2000-2001 CBA season, scouts from the various NBA teams shuttled back and forth to see Yao Ming, to see this Chinese guy who had blocked Vince Carter, the "dunk king," at the Sydney Olympics. Agents David Falk, Bill Duffy, and Matt Sarmen, as well as the assistant general manager of the Washington Wizards and upper-level management personnel of the Philadelphia 76ers and the Orlando Magic all came at one time or another to talk with the Sharks about arrangements for Yao Ming.

What followed was a battle of agents surrounding Yao Ming. Wang Zhizhi's agent Bill Duffy had taken an interest in Yao Ming early on, and David Falk, king of the NBA agents, also announced that he had become Yao Ming's agent and would be responsible for preparing Yao Ming's advance to the NBA.

Falk had been Michael Jordan's and Patrick Ewing's agent, but his wishful thinking angered Yao Ming, who didn't get mad easily. According to NBA regulations, a player's agent was to be chosen solely by the player himself. On March 25, Yao Ming sent a letter to NBA headquarters as a formal statement indicating that before he was drafted, he didn't want anyone to be his agent - which is permitted by the NBA.

Ultimately, Yao Ming did have an agent for going to the NBA, but that was a year later. On May 17, 2002, Yao Ming authorized Erik Mingji Zhang, a cousin, and Professor John Huizinga of the University of Chicago School of Business, to act as his agent and representative.

In hindsight, it was not a bad thing for Yao Ming to have delayed entering the draft for a year, but at the time, Yao Ming was slowly mulling over his inexpressible disappointment. "The NBA has always been the basketball heaven that I have been heading toward; of course it's better to go earlier. Things seemed to go too smoothly for me when I was growing up, almost as though everything had been arranged. But only after you've been disappointed and had the experience of seeing that dream fly away from right in front of you, only then do you truly grow up. From that time on, I learned to be more accepting of things"

So for a while, Yao Ming was downhearted. He would smile for the television cameras, but it was all just a façade.

7. Who Can Compete?

Yao Ming Criticized

"Five fouls before the end of the first half! How can you play the rest of the game? Every time you foul, you affect not only yourself but the rest of the team as well!"

Li Qiuping very seldom yelled at Yao Ming like this.

It was December 29, 1999, the twelfth game of the CBA 1999-2000 season, the Shanghai Sharks hosting the Beijing Shougang Ducks. Against Mengke Bateer, the famous center of the Ducks, Yao Ming made the same mistake that Wang Zhizhi had made that year, jumping up in front of "Big Ba" whenever the opportunity arose to block his shots, knocking them down one after the other. This put Mengke Bateer in a difficult position, and the crowd was in a frenzy, yelling, "Yao Ming, block him!"

On the sidelines, Li Qiuping's eyebrows became more and more furrowed. Once, twice, three times, four times, five times! Although Yao Ming forced Mengke Bateer to retreat, he also got himself in foul trouble. If he fouled once more, he would foul out of the game.

In the first half, the two teams were tied 47 all. During halftime, Li Qiuping jumped all over Yao Ming.

He was Yao Ming's mentor, and it had been he who had brought Yao Ming from the Xu Jia Hui District Youth Sports

School to the Shanghai youth team; who had taken a weak, skinny kid and turned him into a top-ranked center in Asia; but their relationship was more than just "master and disciple." They had been together morning and night for years, had always been open and candid with one another, and although they differed in age by some 20 years, they had established a silent rapport with one another, and at key moments their exchanged glances took the place of yelling and shouting.

In Li Qiuping's eyes, Yao Ming was very "good," which meant not only that he was very sincere and tolerant but also that he handled all kinds of relationships very well, was willing to work very hard in practice, could firmly and fully carry out the orders of the coach during a game, and was very sensible and intelligent; throughout the team, he was very seldom criticized. And his skills were getting better and better: in the first eleven games of the new season, Yao Ming had blocked a total of 70 shots, more than twice as many as Wang Zhizhi.

Although Yao Ming had been playing basketball for several years, Li Qiuping had never seen him so temperamental.

The Beijing Shougang Ducks were a crack team, and the Sharks had lost to them by one point in an away game. This time they were the home team, and since domestic-assistance player Zheng Zhilong was out of the lineup due to injury, if Yao Ming committed another foul and fouled out of the game, they wouldn't have a chance.

Li Qiuping's anger was a wake-up call for Yao Ming at a critical time. When they changed sides and resumed play in the second half, Yao Ming, who had five fouls on him, watched himself with the utmost care and finished the entire game, firmly dominating the boards in both the first and second halves.

This game was won by the Sharks, 88 to 81.

In the 1999-2000 season, the Sharks had the best lineup since the founding of the team. On the one hand, the importation of both domestic and foreign assistance players had been successful. Zheng Zhilong was brought in from Taiwan. Zheng was a high-energy player known as "the Michael Jordan of Taipei" and "the best player in Asia." He was the first player in Taiwan to shatter a backboard while dunking. There were also two foreign-assistance players, Michael Jones and Muntrelle Dobbins, both from America, the former being the current "points king" of the American Youth League. On the other hand, after two seasons of "growth in fierce fire," Yao Ming, Liu Wei, Jia Xiaozhong and the other young worthies were maturing rapidly.

But in the beginning, things did not go smoothly for this fabulous lineup.

Yao Ming later remembers, "At the beginning of the 1999-2000 league games, we were always playing very sloppily, and it's true what some people were saying, that our minds weren't focused enough. But to simply say that 'our minds weren't focused' is not enough. The question is, How come? Was it because our team still lacked a little audacity? During that period when I was injured in the previous season, I was very pessimistic, but then I realized that our team was still playing pretty well, and our lineup at that time was not nearly as good as it is now. So I think that no matter whether we bring in Zheng Zhilong or other good players to assist us in the future, the most important thing is still to establish our own confidence and audacity, because in the end what we must believe in is ourselves."

After successfully moving up from a Class-B to a Class-A team in 1996, the Shanghai Sharks vacillated between 5th and

6th place in the CBA for three seasons; they was often the sub-
jects of criticism, and the club, the coaches, and the players were
all under pressure. Although they now had the best lineup in
their entire history, the Sharks fell into an odd state as soon as
the new season began: they wanted to win and were afraid to
lose, but as soon as they grew hasty, things fell apart and they
lost. And even when they won, Li Qiuping was not satisfied.

Confidence and audacity — this was just the "bottleneck"
where Yao Ming and his teammates urgently needed a
breakthrough.

On January 20, 2000, the Sharks hosted the Rockets, and
the Hu Wan Gymnasium was packed.

Wang Zhizhi scored for the Rockets with a strong post attack to open the contest, and Yao Ming immediately responded
with a two-handed dunk. Nobody really cared which of the
two teams won this game; the main attraction was to see which
of the two giants of Chinese basketball would have a higher level
of performance.

Perhaps because of the enormous pressure of a home game
and the heavy psychological effect of longing to defeat the in-
domitable Rockets, Yao Ming did not put on as good a show as
Wang Zhizhi and didn't experience a top-notch performance as
in other games. The Sharks lost to the Rockets 98 to 119. Of
course, Yao Ming wasn't responsible for the loss, but his performance showed he was in urgent need of mental toughening.

The media's critique of this game said, "Wang Zhizhi and
Yao Ming have already become the two giants of Chinese men's
basketball today. But last night's campaign indicated that the
skills and actual competitive ability of Wang Zhizhi, who has
now competed for several years, have progressed enormously,

and he is unquestionably the number-one center."

Wang Zhizhi's performance during the game was outstanding, and his scoring percentage was very high. During the first two periods, the Rockets led Shanghai 57 to 39. Wang Zhizhi scored 25 points, some 44% of the team's total. Although Yao Ming had four outstanding blocks, his scoring percentage during the first two periods was very low, hardly the equal of Wang Zhizhi.

On April 12, 2000, in the post-season voting by fans to select the best lineup, Wang Zhizhi received 24,736 votes to be chosen center in the best lineup, the other four players chosen for the best lineup being forward Hu Weidong of the Jiangsu Dragons (27,316 votes), forward Sun Jin of the Jilin Northeast Tigers (21,185 votes), guard Li Xiaoyong of the Liaoning Hunters (23,347 votes), and guard Li Qun of the Guangdong Tigers (22,183 votes).

At the time, a second-best CBA lineup was also selected on the basis of the number of votes received by fan letters, which comprised forward Liu Yudong of the BaYi Rockets, forward Gong Xiaobin of the Shandong Bulls, guard Fan Bin of the BaYi Rockets, and guard Jie Sheng of the Zhejiang Horses - and of course, Yao Ming was also included.

He still needed more effort and refining.

Reaching Too High

"That time, we 'reached too high'."

Remembering the first struggle with the Rockets for the championship of the 1999-2000 season, Yao Ming was very happy.

The goal that the Shanghai Sharks had set for the players before the league matches was "keep sixth, struggle for fourth, and go for third," and nobody expected that in post-season play that the Sharks would be "reaching for first" after eliminating the Beijing Ducks 2 to 0 and taking down their "old foe" the Guangdong Tigers 3 to 1.

After playing in the CBA league matches, the Sharks competed with the Rockets a total of eight times but with only one victory. But after every contest, the team seemed to improve, Yao Ming, who entered CBA matches beginning in 1997. What better opponents than the highly skilled assemblage of BaYi team players to promote improvement in one's own skills?

On March 12, 2000, the first game of the final playoff round began in Shanghai.

The Sharks had made full preparations before the game, and the Rockets did not dare to treat the game too lightly, so they had begun to get ready twelve days earlier.

The two teams struggled fiercely during the first period of the game, with Liu Yudong of the Rockets opening the scoring and Wang Zhizhi making a three-pointer right afterwards to lead 5 to 0. The Sharks for the first time put together a lineup consisting of the strong foreign-assistance player Muntrelle Dobbins, Yao Ming, Zhang Wenqi, Zheng Zhilong and Liu Wei. Before the 6-minute mark, Yao Ming on defense successfully blocked the lay-up of the Rockets' Fan Bin, and the play of the whole team rapidly fell into place, with Dobbins scoring under the basket, and they evened the score right away at 14 all. Then Dobbins made a free throw and turned the score around, and the first period ended with them leading 29 to 28. Not long after the second period of the contest had begun, the Sharks' mainstay guard, Liu Wei, twisted his foot and had to come out of the game. He was replaced by Number 4 Liu Peng, which greatly affected the man-to-man offensive and defensive formations, and they didn't score any points for many minutes. The Rockets sent in their old stalwart Ah Dijiang to put together an attack, and the great play of Wang Zhizhi, Liu Yudong, and Li Nan both inside and outside gradually widened the difference between the two teams' scores. By the time the first half was over, the Rockets led by 15 points, 58 to 43. At the start of the second half, the Sharks were counterattacking stubbornly and strongly, but the score kept widening and they grew disheartened and finally totally collapsed, losing to Beijing by a large margin, 94 to 116.

During this game, Yao Ming finally experienced difficulty when "a single log cannot prop up a tottering building." In his solo struggle with the Rockets, the other foreign-assistance players and teammates did not display the same do-or-die fighting spirit that he did. In this game, he made 21 points and got 17 rebounds, but it was not enough to turn the tide.

Image-wise, the Rockets were full of confidence and audacity, their tactical shifts were unfathomable, the players were strongly coordinated, and Wang Zhizhi was always great at inside offense; and deployed his three-point scoring ability. In this game, Wang Zhizhi scored 37 points, including a tally of 3 three-point shots.

On March 15, the Sharks set out for Ningbo to play the Rockets once again.

The game began like the first act of a drama. After the two teams had each scored four points, the Rockets suddenly went "completely cold," and in the next five minutes they were outplayed by the Sharks 16 to 0, and so the "visiting" team, much to everyone's surprise, had now opened a huge lead, 20 to 4. Just when many of the spectators were thinking that the Rockets might lose the second game of the season, the old veteran Li Yudong suddenly exerted himself, scoring seven points in a row and motivating the Rockets, and right away the Rockets' head coach Zhang Bin substituted Ah Dijiang, who was gradually recovering his form, for Fan Bin. In the minutes that followed, the Rockets made up their opponent's 20-to-4 differential, and by the end of the first period the Rockets surpassed their opponent by two points, 26 to 24.

A dramatic scene also occurred in the second period, only the style was different: the electronic scoreboard in the basketball arena suddenly malfunctioned, but this unexpected occurrence didn't affect the game's turning white-hot, with the two teams' opposition and growing ever more fiercely. At the conclusion of this period, the Sharks were leading by one point, 55 to 54.

Because they had not managed to open up a big lead in the first half, the Sharks confidently began the third period by pulling out their "dual foreign-assistance" magic weapon: the lineup on the court was Yao Ming, Zhang Wenqi, and Zheng Zhilong along with Dobbins and Michael Jones, which was by no means inferior to the Rockets' lineup. Then, when the two teams had battled to a 65-65 tie in the third period, the Rockets once again shifted into high gear. Wang Zhizhi suddenly pulled to the outside, scoring repeatedly with medium- and long-range shots. The Rockets went on a small 15-5 run and finally established a double-digit lead. It was this 10-point difference that determined victory and defeat in the game, with the Sharks losing again, 103 to 113. Yao Ming played a full 48 minutes and was completely exhausted after the game. He scored 15 points and grabbed 45 rebounds, and his "sky-net" defense put intense pressure on the Rockets.

This game featured a Bulgarian referee. One of the main reasons for employing foreign referees to referee the games was because the Chinese men's basketball team was about to begin group training in preparation for the Sydney Olympics, and six of the players on the BaYi and Shanghai teams had been selected for the National team, so to have foreign referees governing this match would be beneficial for the Chinese players, as it would allow them to become accustomed to international officiating standards.

March 19, Ningbo, game number three.

The Rockets beat the Sharks 115 to 93, retaining the National League Championship for the fifth time.

The Sharks followed the same old disastrous road. During the first period of the game, they attacked fiercely to take the advantage, and the Rockets' offense was in disarray, strongly attacking beneath the basket to no effect, which gave a big boost to the morale of the Sharks, but they were not tough enough: their skill level fluctuated enormously, and after the Rockets caught up, they became demoralized. At four minutes into the third period they had only scored two points, and in the entire game they had a high number of turnovers, 31. Although Li Qiuping made many substitutions, they still came up short.

Nevertheless, Yao Ming displayed an outstanding mental attitude, and even though he collected three fouls in the first period alone, he still battled courageously despite the pressure, displaying agile footwork and fierce blocking. In this outing he blocked seven shots, had 40 rebounds and scored 29 points, one point more than Wang Zhizhi.

"Even if other clubs paid a high trade fee for me, I wouldn't leave the Shanghai team. I want to help the Shanghai team win the National Class-A League Championship," Yao Ming said after the match. In the short time of only a week, they had played BaYi three times, and although they lost all three contests, Yao Ming's confidence had greatly increased.

On March 22, Shanghai held an awards ceremony for the Sharks, and Yao Ming spoke energetically on behalf of the athletes:

"We have won second place in the league championship which we have long craved, but this is not the final goal of the team. We will continue to exert ourselves to win the overall championship in not too long a time!"

So how long is not too long a time?

Li Qiuping's lips were sealed in this regard, but on the night that the Rockets won their fifth consecutive championship, Li, who was most highly respected even in defeat, said: "The BaYi team, at most, still has two years to dominate the National League Championship."

He said that the Rockets were a superior team, and many of their players were on the National yeam; this was because the teams elsewhere did not enjoy the same good conditions. At present, it would be hard to change this superiority within a short time, but such superior conditions would not last too long, and he estimated that "this team still has two years' time to dominate domestic basketball."

The basis for Li Qiuping's making such a prediction was that, of the mainstays of the BaYi Rockets, Liu Yudong and Fan

Bin, were both over thirty years of age, Ah Dijiang was thirty-three, and high-point man Zhang Jinsong was twenty-eight. These players would at most be able to play for their team in two seasons' worth of league matches. Li Qiuping also clearly felt that, aside from their comparatively good physical condition, the Rockets' bench had no especially outstanding ball skills, and this would weaken their ability to defend their crown.

"The BaYi team's having such superior conditions was created by special circumstances. Their ranks are chosen from among the best talent nationwide, as the teams of the various military regions can send their superior athletes to the BaYi team. Teams elsewhere do not enjoy such special conditions. The Shanghai team can only choose athletes from among a population of 14,000,000, which is clearly far inferior to the situation of the BaYi team," Li Qiuping said. "However, after the founding of the clubs, basketball players from throughout the nation can move freely, and at the same time it is allowed to bring in foreign assistance, which will enormously improve both the situations of local teams and their ability to contend with the BaYi team."

Full Moon Over Sydney

On September 12, 2000, two joyous events occurred for Yao Ming.

That day was the Mid-Autumn Festival, and it was also Yao Ming's 20th birthday. On that same day, he formally registered to become a member of the Chinese basketball team for the 2000 Olympic Games in Sydney, Australia.

Yao Ming and his teammates, who had flown into Sydney that morning, participated in a workout at the domed gymnasium in Olympic Park. After nearly 90 minutes of practice, Xinhua News Agency reporter Xu Jicheng, who had been waiting on the sidelines, wished him a happy birthday. At that time it was 7:30 p.m. local time on the twelfth.

Yao Ming was not the least bit imprecise: "There's still half an hour to go. I won't be 20 for another half hour. I was born at 7 p.m. Beijing time. Sydney is three hours ahead of Beijing, so when it's 9:30 here it should be 6:30 in Beijing."

The first birthday present Yao Ming received was, of course, his athlete's ID badge. From the moment he put on the badge he became an Olympic athlete. That was some eight hours before he became 20, so strictly speaking, Yao Ming became an Olympic athlete at the age of 19, which is the record for youngest in the history of China.

The second birthday gift was placed onto the magazine racks in the Olympic News Center, the Press Village, and the Athletes' Village before Yao Ming had seen it. It was a long article in a special edition of the renowned American sports magazine *Sports Illustrated* about Yao Ming, Wang Zhizhi, and Mengke Bateer, the three big and tall Chinese centers, entitled "The Great Wall." A photograph of Yao Ming alone covered an entire page. The writer, Alex Wolff, pointed out in the article that when photographer Al Tielemans suggested that Yao Ming, Wang Zhizhi, and Mengke Bateer go together to the Great Wall to be photographed, Yao Ming had said, "Is that necessary? When the three of us stand together, *we're* the Great Wall."

The third present that Yao Ming received was the delayed congratulations of his teammates, coaches, and leadership. If the reporter had not mentioned it, even the leader of the Chinese men's basketball team and the manager of the Basketball Management Center, Xin Lancheng, would not have known that the 12th was Yao Ming's birthday. But Yao Ming was truly able to keep it to himself, and so it wasn't until they were having their nighttime snack after evening practice that his teammates wished Yao Ming a happy birthday. That very same night, Xin Lancheng brought a gift from the headquarters of the Chinese delegation to give to Yao Ming on behalf of the team, and Yao Ming invited everyone to eat mooncakes to celebrate the Mid-Autumn Festival together.

To become an Olympian is the common dream of all athletes, and this is especially true for Yao Ming, who bore the disappointments of his father's generation: to participate in the Olympics was even more important than playing in the NBA.

In contrast to the dejection and helplessness of 1998 when he was not chosen for the Asian Games lineup, Yao Ming had come to rely on his actual strength to take control of his own destiny and had become the indisputable mainstay of the men's basketball team of the Chinese Olympics delegation.

The Chinese men's basketball team competing in the Sydney Olympics was under the leadership of Jiang Xingquan, commanding twelve great worthies: Li Qun, Li Xiaoyong, Sun Jun, Hu Weidong, Zhang Jinsong, Li Nan, Liu Yudong, Zheng Wu, Yao Ming, Mengke Bateer, Wang Zhizhi, and Guo Shiqiang.

The Chinese men's basketball team was the only Asian men's basketball team in the Sydney Olympics. Prior to going to Sydney, they participated in a series of warm-up games, first playing two games against the Korean team, and then taking part in the Asian Super League Matches in which the NBA Ambassadors team also participated. In mid-July they had gone to America to conduct a month's worth of training, competing with a number of European and American teams. After returning home in the first part of August, they played three games against the American Dream Team, and from September 2-6 they went to Hong Kong to take part in the Diamond Cup Match, which featured international teams from various continents. This proved to be a valuable test. After playing in the Diamond Cup, the spectacle of the Sydney Olympics formally began.

There were both high- and low-level objectives for these warm-ups, but everyone without exception had nothing but endless praise for Yao Ming.

"In the two games we lost, we lost mainly because of the Chinese team's Yao Ming and the other two big, tall centers; they can attack and defend," said NBA Ambassadors head coach Nate "Tiny" Archibald, Basketball Hall-of-Famer and one of the NBA's 50 Greatest Players. "The physical condition of the Chinese team's inside three big centers would be first-rate even on an NBA team."

The Dream Team composed of NBA superstars was the strongest opponent faced by the Chinese team during the warm-up matches. The Chinese team only won one game in Shanghai on August 17.

That was the third game between the two teams, which the Chinese team won 79 to 60, regaining a little face while at the same time playing a worthwhile warm-up game prior to the Sydney Olympics.

Yao Ming put on a great show in that game, and the superstar NBA Dream Team players found it very difficult to guard him; they pretty much gave up the inside on defense, allowing

Yao Ming to repeatedly pull down offensive rebounds and score, and Yao Ming ended up with 20 points.

During the game with the NBA Ambassadors on the evening of July 3, Yao Ming defended tenaciously, and an impact opened a wound on his lower jaw, requiring five stitches. In a game prior to that, his head was struck at the eyebrow, and blood streamed all over his face. It took ten stitches to close the wound.

During these warm-up games, Yao Ming required more than thirty stitches.

Everybody admired him: "Yao Ming, you're a real hardy boy!"

Yao Ming didn't think it was anything out of the ordinary. "Well, Zhang Jinsong had more than fifty stitches. Compared to him, this is nothing!"

Two Blocks Startle the Dream

Vince Carter, the "slam-dunk king" of the Dream Team, was about to do a signature slam-dunk, but his motion, which should have been uniquely colorful, faltered as the ball was batted away by Yao Ming.

When Carter landed, his face had an astonished expression like he had just encountered an alien from outer space. And for a few short seconds, the Olympic domed arena was also astonished; then Yao Ming was drowned in applause.

On September 17, 2000, the Chinese men's basketball team faced off against the American Dream Team.

This game was the first competition for each of the two teams at the Sydney Olympics. Dream Team head coach Rudy

Tomjanovich sent forth a starting lineup of Jason Kidd, Gary Payton, Kevin Garnett, Vince Carter, and Alonzo Mourning. The head coach of the Chinese team, Jiang Xingquan, dispatched the "twin towers" Yao Ming and Wang Zhizhi, to begin the game.

At the Sydney Olympics, there was only one team bold enough to announce before the games began that it would take the gold medal, and that was Dream Team. Their opponents could not hope for victory, but only for a smaller loss.

Speaking about the Chinese team before the game, Carter was especially boastful: "How to play the Chinese team? We treat all teams the same. The big guy? 7'6"? I have dunked over the head of a 7'7" player before. The key to the game of basketball is not height."

Coach Tomjanovich also appeared relaxed before the game: "I have never seen any of the Chinese team's games or video tape, I've only heard that they are very tall, and that's all I know."

A reporter asked, "Would you like to go to China to train these tall young kids?"

Tomjanovich started to show off his own sense of humor: "I would prefer going to China to eat Chinese food. Their being so tall must have something to do with eating Chinese food. After I go back home, I'm going to have my son eat Chinese food. He's already 17 and only 6'4"."

During the pre-game warm-up, the Dream Team seemed nonchalant. Before the players went onto the court, the court announcer first asked the spectators a question: "Who is the world's tallest center?" As a roar arose in the stands, the large video monitor flashed Yao Ming's name and the spectators grew very excited, and when Yao Ming ran out onto the court surrounded by his teammates, the entire arena rocked with cheers and the bleachers were filled with camera flashes.

The Dream Team didn't want Yao Ming to steal their thunder, and during pre-game practice they began to stir up the spectators' emotions. They didn't just shoot orderly baskets like the Chinese players; rather, they playfully put on a show, with flying dunks and alley-oops.

However, the first five minutes of the game belonged to the Chinese team, as they led most of the time 13 to 7.

"Their performance really startled us. Of course, at the beginning we were a bit sluggish, but we are not always like that. Five minutes into the game, we were always trailing. This was sort of unimaginable," said Gary Payton.

Most of the Dream Team's offensive plays were concentrated under the basket, their effectiveness based on getting the ball to Alonzo Mourning, but with Yao Ming's blocking, Mourning's offense seemed sloppy, and there was little outstanding play under the basket. The Chinese team counterattacked incessantly, and there were two great plays repeated when Wang Zhizhi got the defensive rebound and passed the ball out rapidly and Yao Ming received the ball and scored with a lay-up.

What shocked the Dream Team was Yao Ming's towering hands, which blocked the American players twice in succession, first Garnett and then Carter. The Sydney *Daily Telegraph* of September 18 described it thusly: "When Yao Ming blocked Payton's shot out of the court, it was like swatting a mosquito."

Then it was as though the Dream Team suddenly awoke. These top-notch NBA players brought their experience to bear, and with two or three flowery passes and alley-oop dunks, they rapidly upset the Chinese team's formations and then adopted the method of forcing Yao Ming and Wang Zhizhi to commit fouls, dismantling the effectiveness of their play. Wang Zhizhi already had four fouls before seven minutes of the first half, and the coach had to take him out. With two minutes to go in the first half, Yao Ming and Mengke Bateer had four fouls apiece, and not long after the beginning of the second half, Yao Ming had to leave the game because he had accumulated five fouls, and then all he could do was watch from the bench. Yao Ming had scored a total of five points and gotten three rebounds.

"I had waited a very long time for that game, and I'm very satisfied with my performance," Yao Ming said afterwards.

Although the Chinese team lost the game 72 to 119, the performance of the entire Chinese team was very satisfactory.

Dream Team Coach Tomjanovich began to take notice of Yao Ming and the others: "These young guys on the Chinese team will have a boundless future."

Carter, who had been repeatedly blocked by Yao Ming, was somewhat sour; he said he didn't know who it was that blocked him, that he never remembered the opponents' names, and that he only played for the fun of it. When asked whether Yao Ming's defense had posed a threat to his dunking, Carter shrugged his shoulders, shook his head, and said, "That's how the game of basketball goes, I don't care who blocked me." But he felt that the "big boys" of the Chinese team performed very bravely: "They were fearless, not afraid of anybody. They were really into it, and this is the kind of opponent I like to compete with, 'cause it makes the game more fun."

Mourning heaped heavy praise on Yao Ming: "He is really talented. Seldom do you have somebody who is tall like him and fast at the same time; he's a genius. He's only 20, and he can pass and also shoot. But he has to work on his strength and put on some weight, and learn a lot of basic skills. If only he is willing to work hard, he will certainly be able to succeed. I hope that in the future I will be able to compete with Yao Ming in the NBA."

Portland Trailblazers sharpshooter Steve Smith also said, "Yao Ming should play in the NBA, I really like his skills. He has strong running and jumping ability, and the Trailblazers need players like this."

After the game, Yao Ming was besieged by the press. He said that he didn't think he would foul out so soon: "We played very relaxed today, and we didn't think we would play so well in the opening stage of the game. But there's still a big difference between us and the NBA. Anybody can be blocked, because the height of the rim isn't going to change, but the refs just called too many fouls on us, and there was nothing we could do. All we can do is to improve our blocking skills in the future."

In the games which followed, the Chinese men's basketball team defeated the New Zealand team 75 to 60, lost to the French team 70 to 82, lost to the Lithuanian team 66 to 82, beat the Italian team 85 to 76, and lost to the Spanish team 64 to 84. With two victories and four losses in six contests, they earned tenth place in men's basketball at the Sydney Olympics.

Although their achievement was not as good as the eighth place at the Atlanta Olympics four years earlier, the Chinese men's basketball team-and Yao Ming-attracted far more attention. Yao Ming not only had the advantages of height and age, but he was also very agile, and his footwork, dunking, and rebounding all showed how unusually supple his body was.

This Chinese man who had just passed his 20th birthday was lauded as "the greatest discovery in the world of basketball."

NBA superstar Bill Walton said, "Yao Ming will change the way basketball is played."

Yao Ming also remembers that at the Sydney Olympics, he gained greater self-confidence.

On September 25, just as the game between the Chinese team and the Italian team was approaching the ending buzzer, NBA Commissioner David Stern made a special trip to the Olympic Village to visit Yuan Weimin, head of the National Sports Ministry, chairman of the Chinese Olympics Committee, and leader of the Chinese Olympic Delegation.

Stern indicated that he was extraordinarily willing to provide assistance and promote more matches between the Chinese teams and NBA teams. "However, I must make it clear that I am not here to 'kidnap' Yao Ming and Wang Zhizhi. I hope that in the future if they want to play in the NBA they will receive the agreement and support of the Chinese sports leadership. If Chinese players can go to the NBA to play, then it will be a lot more convenient if they want to return to China to play in the Asian Games, the Olympic Games, and World Championship matches, and this way the level of Chinese and Asian basketball will be improved."

Yuan Weimin expressed that in the future China would have players who go to play in the NBA, but that it would take time.

At a special press conference for the Xinhua News Agency and China Central Television which followed, Stern said that after watching the game between the Chinese team and the American team, this is what he thought: "If the Chinese team can improve their training, for example, by increasing the content of and equipment for strength training, the Chinese team could very well win the Olympic prize in another four years. I hope that NBA players will in the future be able to play for their home countries. I also hope that Chinese players will raise their level and join the NBA, and then go back to play for China in the Asian Games and the Olympics. This is our goal."

In Sydney, as far as Yao Ming was concerned, joining the NBA was already a dream that was gradually growing clearer day by day. The Americans began to remember the height, ball skills, and also the humor of this remarkable player.

After the game with the Dream Team, an American reporter asked Yao Ming, "What's the secret of how you grew so tall?"

He answered laughingly, "Because I get more fresh air up here."

8.   Growing Up and Coming of Age

"We've Grown Up!"

In the 1999-2000 CBA season, the Shanghai Sharks had unexpectedly won the silver medal, and Yao Ming laughingly referred to it as "reaching too far." For 2000-2001, the Sharks had already become the greatest opponent of the BaYi Rockets, the defending champions.

On November 18, 2000, the inaugural contest of this season was a clash between the Sharks and the Rockets, with both teams fully utilizing their core players to start. Yao Ming began the scoring with a two-pointer and a long three-point shot, while Wang Zhizhi was listless and weak on offense, and even though Li Nan scored repeatedly with his signature "flying knife" long shots, the Rockets lost 96 to 101.

After getting off to a good start, the Sharks went on to play like a hot knife through butter, setting a record for eleven consecutive victories, and the Rockets clearly deteriorated, losing three games on the road and dropping down to the middle ranks.

This lasted until the December 31 match, deemed the "battle of the century," held in Ningbo, in which the Rockets won a major victory over the Sharks, 117 to 91.

In this contest Wang Zhizhi once again vied with Yao Ming for supremacy, scoring 26 points and making three dunks and three blocks. Yao Ming, who played three fewer minutes, scored 18 points and had one dunk and four blocks. With the close of the century and the millennium, both teams eagerly anticipated their future matches in the post-season.

March 11, Shanghai.

The Rockets were ahead in the first period. As soon as the game began, the Sharks sent in their "all-star" lineup, basically assuming a defensive posture and fighting hard to reduce the gap, but the difference in the two teams' scores reached 10 to 20 at one point. But through its all-out efforts, the Sharks closed the gap to 29 to 33. The goal of the Sharks was very clear, namely, to shut down Li Nan and gather their strength before going on the offensive again. In the contests between the two teams during the regular season, no matter whether the home team won or the visiting team lost, Li Nan was always an enormous threat to the Sharks. But in this game, Li Nan was basically "frozen," and in the entire game he made only two of eight three-point shots and four out of ten two-point shots, scoring only 16 points for a scoring percentage of only 25%.

During the second period, the Sharks were forced into sending in a second center replace Jia Xiaozhong, unlike their usual practice of first sending in a guard. This tactic was very astute, the goal being to further expand their inside advantage and continue to constrict Wang Zhizhi's room to move on the inside, and the Sharks' situation gradually took a turn for the better. Shan Weiguo's basket tied the game for the first time at 49, and since Li Nan had been shut down, Liu Yudong began to liven it up outside, but this led to the Rockets being hard-pressed inside. Wang Zhizhi was just ordinary beneath the basket, but in trying to resist Yao Ming, he was at a height disadvantage and tended to commit more fouls.

At the end of the first half, the Sharks trailed by four points, 59 to 63.

In the second half, the Sharks remained at a disadvantage, and the gap in the score grew to 10 at one point. Yao Ming also missed two free throws. Not long after, Wang Zhizhi committed a defensive foul against Yao Ming, and Yao Ming made the free throws, so the score was 79 to 82, but Wang Zhizhi had fouled five times, so Wang Fei had no choice but to take him out of the game.

Wang Zhizhi's leaving the game became the turning point deciding the advantage of the two teams, and a key three-pointer by Shan Weiguo allowed the Sharks to turn the score around for the first time, 83 to 82. However, at that time, the Sharks' power forward, Zhang Wenqi, was taken out because he had fouled five times, and so for the first time they had three guards in the game. The final score for the third period was 86 all.

In the last period, when Shan Weiguo put the home team ahead 92 to 90 with another three-pointer, the Rockets sent Wang Zhizhi back in. When the Sharks were leading 105 to 99, the Rockets missed the shot clock twice on offense. The home team took advantage of the opportunity to increase their advantage, and with 43 seconds remaining, the Sharks led 112 to 105.

Yao Ming walked to the backcourt, raised his hands toward the fans, and made a victory sign. The Sharks won their home game against the Rockets, thus ending the "legend" of the BaYi team's never losing a post-season game since the establishment of the CBA.

This victory by the Sharks in the first game of the postseason was half due to the defense against Li Nan. Before the game, Li Qiuping's last words of instruction to the players were: "Cover Li Nan and don't let him shoot three-pointers." Throughout the game, the Sharks utilized Yao Ming to hold the advantage inside while effectively shutting down Li Nan's long three-point shots outside.

The credit for silencing Li Nan doesn't belong to anybody in particular but rather to the efforts of the team as a whole. Although Liu Wei had the main responsibility on the court for guarding Li Nan, almost every player of the Sharks double-teamed Li Nan, including Yao Ming, the center, deep inside, who often came out to supplement the defense and didn't even hesitate to fall down in order to prevent Li Nan from having comfortable shots. In the entire first half, Li Nan didn't make a single three-point shot; he simply didn't have much chance to shoot at all.

March 14, Ningbo, the next battle.

The game started at 7:35 p.m., and Yao Ming was first to score four points, to which Wang Zhizhi responded with a three-pointer from outside. However, this three-pointer was to be Wang Zhizhi's only score in the first period. When the Rockets were leading by 20 to 15, the Sharks went on a 9 to 0 run to reverse the score and lead by four points. In the first period, the Sharks led the Rockets by three points, 30 to 27. In this period, Liu Yudong showed why he was irreplaceable, scoring 16 points; more than half the team's point total was scored by Liu.

After the second period began, the Sharks retained the advantage, widening the scoring gap to 8 points, at which time

Wang Fei put in Liu Qiang for Wang Zhizhi and began to full-court press. Li Nan, who had just gone into the game, began to demonstrate his uniqueness by racking up some three-pointers, and the two teams battled to a 45-all tie. Then the Rockets resolutely intensified their outside defense with the intention of cutting off the Sharks' inside-outside connection, relying on three-pointers from the perimeter to score again and again. This shift put the Sharks at a loss, and a 9-0 run by the Rockets put them in the lead at the close of the first half, 58 to 51.

When the second half began, the Sharks sent in their two foreign-assistance players, and by then Yao Ming already had five fouls, so he was being overly cautious on defense. The Rockets seized the opportunity and put Wang Zhizhi back in, hoping to take further advantage of Yao Ming and force him to foul for the sixth time. Before the third period was half over, the Rockets were already leading their opponent by more than 16 points.

In previous games, a 16-point lead would almost certainly have guaranteed a win for the Rockets, but after the first contest, the Sharks had begun to show dominance, shrinking the scoring gap to only three points. When the fourth period began, the Sharks' continued to play impressively, and within two minutes the score was unexpectedly tied at 96 all. The atmosphere in the arena reached a peak of excitement, and the roaring of the crowd was deafening. From 96 all the two teams played to 108 to 107, with the Rockets leading by one point.

Then, with less than two minutes left in the game, the Sharks put together a successful defense, and almost at the precise moment when the buzzer on the shot clock sounded, Fan Bin shot and scored from outside the three-point line; it was this three-pointer that would clinch the Rockets' victory. With 16 seconds remaining, the Rockets led by two points, 111 to 109. But the Rockets had possession, and it was then that Li Nan shot and scored the final three-point shot.

The Rockets won by a narrow margin, 114 to 109.

Even though they had won the game, the BaYi players broke out in a cold sweat: the Sharks were simply amazing. Before, they had only been able to make up a scoring deficit of ten points or so in the fourth period, and they had never before seen the Shanghai players fight their way back again and again. The Sharks team of today was so much like the Rockets of yesterday.

Without a doubt, the biggest improvement on the Shanghai team was Yao Ming. Li Nan, master of the outside attack, also felt Yao Ming's prowess: "I really didn't expect Yao Ming to have improved so much this year. Now all the Shanghai team needs is Yao Ming on the inside, and because of Yao Ming's superiority under the basket, the other players can relax and go out to guard Fan Bin and me on the perimeter. Offensively, Yao Ming ties up a lot of our defensive strength, and everybody else pulls out to the perimeter, which puts a lot of pressure on our outside."

March 18, Ningbo, the next match.

Yao Ming went onto the court bandaged up, and this game was more sedate than usual.

During practice in the afternoon of March 17, Yao Ming bumped, was opening a gash at the corner of his eye: He bled all over the court.

Team leader Yu Xiaomiao was taking him to the hospital, and after walking a few steps, Yao Ming turned and told Li

Qiuping: "Coach Li, don't worry. I want to keep playing in the game tonight." He got six stitches at the Li Hui Li Hospital in Ningbo.

At the beginning of the game, the Rockets enjoyed a good start through the teamwork of Wang Zhizhi and Zhang Jinsong. But the good situation didn't last long, as Yao Ming's strong inside defensive strength caused repeated turnovers by the Rockets, and there were two blocks by Yao Ming that especially aroused the spirits of the Shanghai players. During the first period of the game, the Sharks led the Rockets by two points.

When Li Nan went onto the court in the second period, the play of the BaYi team gradually underwent some subtle changes, with Wang Zhizhi pulling out more to the perimeter to avoid being cut off by Yao Ming. Wang, Zhang Jinsong, and Li Nan all scored from outside the three-point line, instantly reversing the score. Throughout this period of the game, the Rockets resolutely played an outside strategy, and the three-point shots of Li Nan and Zhang Jinsong were so accurate beyond belief. Soon, the Rockets had attained a seven-point advantage.

At the conclusion of the third period, the Rockets and the Sharks had 96 and 94 points, respectively, and the magnitude of both teams' firepower had never before been seen in their previous games. When the fourth period began, the two teams' scores were still very close, and the atmosphere on the court grew more and more tense. But when the Rockets took the lead 104 to 102, some of the Sharks suddenly found it difficult to maintain self-control, and many single-player or 'one-on-one' attacks began happening, so Yao Ming's advantage was not being fully utilized. The experienced Rockets seized this opportunity to go on a 10-to-0 run to widen their advantage. Before the game ended, the

Sharks, knowing that they had been bested again, displayed the style of a CBA professional team. Even until the last second they kept adjusting their tactics, closing the scoring gap one point at a time. With 21 seconds remaining in the game, there was suddenly a problem with the game clock, which wasn't stopped during a free throw and thus ran off an additional ten seconds. At that point, the Rockets were leading, 129 to 121. Yao Ming realized what had happened, and immediately went to the referees' table to mention it. So the game was temporarily halted while the game clock was reset.

Following this game, no one dared to say whether the Sharks would be able to stand up to the Rockets; their only experience was losing.

The Rockets won again, 131 to 122.

Yao Ming pointed to the bandage wrapped around his head and said jokingly, "This is one of the magnificent scenic highlights in the CBA."

March 21, Shanghai, the last game.

This contest was do or die for the Sharks. In the beginning, they had momentum, and Yao Ming made two mid-range shots, which he rarely took; and then he unexpectedly dribbled all the way down the court, a rare sight. Although the Sharks trailed at one time by eight points, at the end of the first period the score was 27 to 28, and they were behind by only one point.

The score remained very close until the middle of the second period, at which time Li Qiuping took out several of his core players, who were replaced by Liu Zhen and the others. They made a lot of turnovers, and the home team's situation rapidly deteriorated. Li Qiuping was thinking he could use the strength of the bench players, not that they would falter here. The second half of the period was almost a one-man struggle by Yao Ming, and the BaYi Rockets ended the first half of the contest leading 64 to 49.

Of the seven three-point baskets in the third period, six were by the Rockets, including Wang Zhizhi, Liu Yudong, and Li Nan. The Sharks' outside game was slow and they were unable to achieve an optimal state, and they were also unable to defend against the opponent's outside game; all they could do was to watch their opponent's demonstration of skills. Four minutes before the end of the period, Li Qiuping took Yao Ming out of the game in order to conserve his strength.

When the fourth period began, the Sharks trailed the Rockets by 20 points, 79 to 99. The result had already been determined, but the Shanghainese — even though they could not turn defeat into victory — turned the last twelve minutes into one of the classic battles in the history of Chinese basketball through a consummate display of skill.

The Sharks, which for the first three periods had been unable to solve the problem of defense, expanded their man-to-man coverage zone as soon as they came out. After successfully thwarting several of the Rockets' offensive plays, foreign-assistance player Damon Stringer worked together with Yao Ming, who had come into the game again, in a matching rhythm, and in a very short time the score difference shrank to 93 to 101, just an 8-point difference. During that stage, Stringer himself scored 11 points, including two three-pointers. For the short period of 3 minutes and 5 seconds, the Shanghai team went on a 14-to-2 run.

Right away, Wang Fei called a time-out and put Wang Zhizhi back in. He didn't try to go head to head with Yao Ming, but rather continued firing from outside and making three three-point shots; it was almost as though he had divine assistance, and every time he scored it was just as the Shanghai team was about to narrow the gap. Wang Zhizhi, who had been brilliantly blocked by Yao Ming during the season, finally gave the Sharks the spear to the throat.

The Sharks lost to the Rockets, 118 to 128.

For two seasons they were second place, but this second place far surpassed that of the previous season.

The game put a period to the end of the 2000-2001 season, a period permeated with the joys and excited tears of growing up and coming of age.

That night, at the Shanghai Hu Wan Gymnasium, it was an evening with complex interwoven emotions.

Wang Zhizhi delightedly hoisted high the championship trophy, realizing the Rockets' sixth consecutive championship.

Yao Ming put his silver medal on his mother, Fang Fengdi, and mother and son embraced tightly. Fang Fengdi said, "Yao Ming did his utmost."

With tears running down his cheeks, Yao Ming said, "We've grown up!"

Centers Face Off

Although the Shanghai Sharks had lost once again to the BaYi Rockets and were once again defeated in their bid for the championship, head coach Li Qiuping could say with pride: "Yao

Ming has already surpassed Wang Zhizhi to become the number one center in China and even in Asia."

"When fine jade has been created, how is it to become brilliant?" When Yao Ming first emerged on the scene, Wang Zhizhi realized that this was the opponent that fate had ordained for him.

In 2000, Wang Zhizhi was touted as "Asia's best center"; that was the zenith of his career. One year later, he began gradually to disappear — eclipsed in the brilliance of the rapidly rising Yao Ming.

In the 2000-2001 season, Yao Ming finally caught up with and supplanted Wang Zhizhi; and this was Wang's final shot, because he went to the NBA the following season.

The transition had actually begun with the first game of the season.

As the opening contest between the Sharks and the Rockets unfolded, Yao Ming scored 22 points while Wang Zhizhi scored only 12. After the match, the Rockets' head coach Wang Fei expressed his dissatisfaction with Wang Zhizhi: "He had trouble utilizing his offensive skills, and his performance was not up to par."

However, the true showdown between Yao Ming and Wang Zhizhi didn't come in a regulation game but rather in four rounds of post season playoff games between the two teams.

After these four contests, although the Sharks were defeated by the Rockets in three games out of four, the 20-year-old Yao Ming had already proven his incontestable superiority beneath the basket. Players and coaches alike all recognized this fact.

After the first playoff game, Li Qiuping said, "Yao Ming's ability beneath the basket has already surpassed Wang Zhizhi's, and inside you'd have to say that Yao Ming is a bit better than he is. In this game, Yao Ming played successfully against Wang several times beneath the basket, but how many times did Wang play directly against Yao Ming beneath the basket? And how many times did he succeed?"

In the second playoff game, Wang Zhizhi could not withstand Yao Ming's inside defense, and many times he pulled out to the outside to shoot three-pointers. Although he was too far away for Yao Ming to help, still Yao Ming now ruled the inside. Following the rise of Yao Ming, Wang Zhizhi's status drifted further and further toward second-best center.

In fact, the Rockets' main player in this game wasn't Wang Zhizhi but Liu Yudong, who single-handedly scored 43 points and became the Sharks' nightmare.

In the third contest, Wang Zhizhi conversely had the upper hand. He no longer behaved like a headstrong child, stubbornly insisting on vying with Yao Ming beneath the basket despite his clear height disadvantage of 3.9" to Yao Ming. In this game, he gave up shifting step by step under the basket with his back to Yao Ming; more often he would take a big step and turn, and this simple evasive move would create a scoring opportunity for him. When the Rockets were on the offense in the first period of the game, except for one time when Wang Zhizhi went up against Yao Ming for a shot and missed, the next five offensive plays were all successful. He penetrated, he rebounded, and he made three-pointers, and in the first period he scored 13 points.

What was even more amazing was that what Wang Zhizhi did best in this game was not offense but defense. Previously, Yao Ming had had a very clear advantage over Wang Zhizhi beneath the basket, and his one-on-one success rate was very high. Formerly, when Wang Zhizhi defended against Yao Ming he would try to take him down right away and not let Yao Ming score or get the offensive rebound, but the more urgent he became, the more he ended up allowing his opponent to score.

But in this game, Wang Zhizhi relied more often on his teammates for defensive help to double-team Yao Ming, while he only paid heed to defending his own position. As a result, Yao Ming had more turnovers in this game and the Sharks' inside offense was weakened.

In the third game, Wang Zhizhi scored 28 points, the first time in the playoffs that his point total exceeded Yao Ming's. He made three out of five three-pointers and had 12 rebounds. No wonder Coach Wang Fei in a post-game critique of his performance said, "Big Zhi played smart ball today."

After the game, Yao Ming also, "Today I'm happy for Big Zhi; he played with a lot of audacity."

With the conclusion of the 2000-2001 season, however, Yao Ming emerged as the biggest winner, individually winning awards in five categories: "regular season MVP", "League MVP", "King of the boards", "King of the dunk," and "King of the block."

And Wang Zhizhi didn't win a single one.

As far as Wang was concerned, things had never been bleaker. In the Men's basketball Final Eight in 1994-1995, Wang Zhizhi came in first in the dunking category. At that time, Yao Ming had just joined the Shanghai youth team not long before, and the Shanghai Sharks had not yet been established. In the 1995-1996 season, Wang won the "King of the dunk" and "King of the block" laurels. In the 1998-1999 season, Yao Ming had begun to make a name for himself, coming in second in blocking, after Wang, but also being chosen as "most valuable defensive player." In the 1999-2000 season, Wang was even more pleased with himself, having won glory as league MVP, but Yao Ming had already pocketed the awards for rebounds, dunks, and blocks, having gotten 116 more rebounds, nine more dunks, and 56 more blocks than Wang Zhizhi. But Yao Ming had scored 114 fewer points than Wang.

Yao Ming was chosen as "best center" for the first time in the voting to select the ideal lineup for this season, and for the first time he got more votes than Wang Zhizhi.

Ever since his debut, and especially after suffering at the hands of Yu Leping of the Zhejiang team, Yao Ming had been pondering how to handle opposing centers. In the beginning, he studied Wang Zhizhi, and he ended by summarizing how to play Wang Shouqiang, Ma Jian, and others; then he discovered that the hardest man to play against was not Wang Zhizhi but Mengke Bateer.

He divided his Chinese opponents into three types. The first type was Liaoning's Wang Shouqiang, Beijing Aoshen's Ma Jian, and others who were not that tall but who had bulk and agile footwork. The second type were the Ducks' Mengke Bateer and Zhejiang's Yu Leping and others who were a bit shorter, had plenty of bulk, but no agile footwork. The third type was Wang Zhizhi, whose feet moved with agility and whose height was pretty close, but who didn't weigh enough.

In previous games, Yao Ming had been bested by centers of the first type, but now he said he believed that his offensive and defensive strength was stronger than theirs. As for Wang Zhizhi, Yao Ming's experience was that Big Zhi had more offensive techniques than he did, so he couldn't just butt heads with him but had to use his brain, by employing more techniques like hook shots or fade-away shots, for example. The game on December 31, 2000, in which the Sharks lost to the Rockets, was the first time in the season that Yao Ming used a hook shot, and the ball went in! Although the shot didn't count because he had been fouled beforehand by the opponent, when he looked carefully at the video later on, he saw that the movements of his whole technique were very connected, and so he decided to resume — and perfect — this type of activity that he had practiced so hard before.

Yao Ming felt that the hardest center to handle was Mengke Bateer: "Bateer is the type whose strength and weight match each other. In playing against Bateer under the basket, I can very clearly feel his strength, and if I let down for just an instant, or even lose my focus, it really affects being able to get a shot off. In playing against Yu Leping, I could easily evade him, but it's very hard to evade Bateer. Sometimes my foot has already moved over but my waist lags behind. And Bateer uses his elbows extremely well; I call it 'crosswise controlling the length'. Actually, the principle is very simple: I don't weigh enough."

But Yao Ming also saw his own advantage. He made an analogy: "Bateer is like a tree, which is incomparably solid at the base, but if it really gets knocked down, then it is very hard to stand upright again; whereas I am like a length of bamboo that bends easily when impacted but can snap back."

Insufficient strength has always been Yao Ming's "Achilles heel." Perhaps those who don't understand basketball would think on first seeing Yao Ming that he is too thin. But insiders all know that Yao Ming's skills are extraordinarily good, especially considering his height and age. Li Qiuping's assessment of Yao Ming's skills is as follows: "Even some of the NBA players are not as good as Yao Ming skill wise. Yao can shoot, pass, has pretty good speed, and he can go to the basket. Many people who have seen Yao Ming shoot have been really surprised that such a tall player has such an unexpectedly good wrist touch!"

At the time, the American ESPN magazine had this assessment of Yao Ming: "For the past decade or so, the NBA has overemphasized strong players, yet during the same period, the international trend has remained skillful play. Yao Ming is the only person who can build a bridge between skills and strength. . . . If Yao Ming can build up his strength, that plus his skills will give him an opportunity to change the development of the entire basketball movement."

Yao Ming says that he understands this principle: "I also want to develop my strength, but there's nothing I can do, I just haven't made it to that level. I will work hard."

Actually, Yao Ming has been working hard all along. On average, he has three strength training sessions per week, including weight training, lifting over and over again, not stopping until he has done the specified amount of sets.

The "Three Tenors"

The men's basketball finals of the Ninth National Games held in Guangzhou at the end of 2001 became the last match-up of Yao Ming, Wang Zhizhi, and Mengke Bateer in China.

It had been seven years since the birth of the Chinese Basketball Association.

Four years earlier, when the Eighth National Games had been held in Shanghai, the CBA had been about to begin its third season, and Yao Ming with his meager physique was about to enter everyone's field of vision. During the last four years, the CBA has enabled Yao Ming, Wang Zhizhi, and Mengke Bateer to become household names, and these three big centers have raised the overall appeal of the whole league, promoted the development of the professional sports market in China, and pushed Chinese basketball out into the world at large.

Although Mengke Bateer, who had returned from training with the Denver Nuggets, had grown a bit thinner, he still had that same level of audacity. He led the Beijing team to a powerful defeat of the Zhejiang team, 78 to 62, scoring a game-high 24 points. Next was the Liaoning team, with Bateer showing his strength under the basket and scoring 31 points, and the Beijing team easily taking its second victory in a row. Although his performance in four strong games for the Beijing team was not the best, his defects did not obscure his virtues, and his skillful moves and three-point skills had obviously improved a great deal.

Wang Zhizhi, who had the benefit of playing in the NBA the previous season, had clearly become quite a bit more robust. In the game between the Liberation Army team and the Tianjin team, Wang Zhizhi was only on the court for 29 minutes and easily scored 36 points. He was first in rebounds, assists and dunks, and he also had no turnovers or fouls; such a performance brought cheers from the spectators. In the game in which the Rockets won a large victory over the Zhejiang team, 117 to 77, Wang Zhizhi was on the court 20 minutes and scored 28 points, without turnovers or fouls. His outstanding play again gave rise to a high tide of cheers from the fans.

Yao Ming was even more the spirited personage that the Shanghai team could not do without. At the Eighth National

Games four years earlier, Yao Ming first played in adult matches, and after several games, he was exhausted. The public took the Shanghai team to task for "pulling the seedling." But for four years, Yao Ming had experienced CBA league matches, the Asian Championship, the East Asian Games, the Olympics, and the World Collegiate Sports Meet, and had experienced delight, anger, sorrow, and happiness on countless occasions. So in reminiscing about the situation during the Eighth National Games four years earlier, Yao Ming no longer remembers very clearly those times that made him so excited.

"At the time of the Eighth National, I was only 17 and weighed 205 lbs. When I was younger, I probably grew about 1.9" a year, but in these past four years I've 'only' grown 2.3"! But if you really want to talk about what kind of changes I've had these past four years, it's here (pointing to his head). Four years ago, I was happy just to be able to play; how could I have dared to hope for anything more? Let alone the NBA. And now, for all the Chinese, instead of being distant and unreachable, the NBA has come to be right in front of us, and to go there and refine myself has become my greatest goal at present. Yes, the ways of the world are hard to predict."

In the first contest of the Ninth National Games, the Shanghai team encountered that "old snake" the Guangdong team. Would the "strong dragon" be able to control the "old snake?" It would depend on Yao Ming's performance, and it turned out that Yao Ming had a magnificent game, and in one fell swoop he racked up 44 points, not only leading the Shanghai team to a 91-to-66 throttling of the host team but also setting a new single-game personal scoring record.

Everyone was looking forward to the second clash of the

Sharks and the Rockets in 2001.

At 8 o'clock in the evening of November 14, the men's basketball playoffs began at the Dong Wan Gymnasium in Guangdong.

The Sharks fielded the same starting lineup as in the previous few games, which included the four veterans Yao Ming, Zhang Wenqi, Jia Xiaozhong, and Liu Wei, as well as a newcomer, Hai Rui, who had been performing remarkably well. But the Rockets' starters were more changed from those in the semi-final match: in addition to the essential Wang Zhizhi, Li Nan, and Chen Ke, previous starters Liu Yudong and Zhou Xinxin were now replaced by Fan Bin and Mo Ke.

But those expecting a final "showdown" between Yao Ming and Wang Zhizhi in China were disappointed: the two didn't play hard against one another beneath the basket for very long. This was Li Qiuping's tricky strategy of coming out ahead by taking advantage of a deliberate mismatch. Although both Yao Ming and Wang Zhizhi appeared in the teams' starting lineups, at the beginning of the game the two of them didn't line up against one another. The Shanghai team had power forward Jia Xiaozhong guard Wang Zhizhi, and Yao Ming went to guard Mo Ke. After the game, Li Qiuping explained that this was a defensive tactic that he was satisfied with: "Wang Zhizhi is both tall and mobile, as well as an accurate three-point shooter. If Yao Ming guarded him he would get pulled outside and be at a disadvantage, so we had Jia Xiaozhong guard Wang Zhizhi, and if he suddenly broke inside, then Yao Ming could come to the rescue on defense. Today when Jia Xiaozhong was guarding Wang Zhizhi, he didn't make many baskets one-on-one!" In the first period, when Wang Zhizhi offensively went directly against

Yao Ming, the two of them only battled twice, and when Yao Ming was on offense he mainly fed his teammates on the side and was in no hurry to go it alone under the basket.

Once into the second period, Yao Ming began to intentionally play under the basket, and in defending him one-on-one, Wang Zhizhi rapidly drew his third personal foul. Wang Fei hurriedly switched Mo Ke to guard Yao Ming, thus further reducing the probability of face-to-face confrontation between the two centers. Later, the Rockets simply substituted Liu Yudong for Wang Zhizhi, and thus Yao Ming became the sole protagonist in this clash of the titans. When Wang Zhizhi came on the court in the second half, the Shanghai team's defensive tactic was as before, with Jia Xiaozhong guarding Wang Zhizhi. Wang Zhizhi only scored 17 points in this game.

But the Rockets did not consist of Wang Zhizhi only. As Yao Ming said after the game, "We lost because we didn't have as many talented players as the Rockets."

In the showdown between Yao Ming and Wang Zhizhi, Liu Yudong ended up playing the leading role.

In the opening stage of this playoff game, the Sharks perilously lost momentum and played very haphazardly, and their opponents intercepted several passes. After six minutes, the Shanghai team trailed the Rockets by more than 12 points.

But starting in the second period, the tenacity and audacity of the Shanghai team gradually began to show; revitalized and reanimated, they flourished both inside and outside, unceasingly narrowing the score, and when the first half ended, the Sharks trailed the Rockets by one point. But several times in the second half when they had gone ahead and wanted to extend their lead, the Shanghai team had some turnovers caused by being too hasty, and at the conclusion of the third period, the Shanghai team still trailed by one point, 69 to 70.

One minute before the end of the fourth period, the Shanghai team's Jia Xiaozhong made a mid-range shot, and the two sides had battled to 88 all. The spectators were all on their feet, and in the stands, which had just a moment before been bubbling over with the clamor of voices, there was now nothing but silence.

At this moment of life and death, the Shanghai team found itself unable to get two defensive rebounds.

They were so close to the championship. With only 1 second remaining, Liu Yudong shot from beyond the three-point line, and just as the referee's whistle blew, the ball went in.

Just a moment before, the taste of victory had been close enough to reach out and touch, but in an instant it had vanished to the far ends of the earth. Having expended all thought and concern, the dreams fell through again, and the jaunty Li Qiuping had now suddenly aged considerably, his hands trembling as he lit a cigarette. Jia Xiaozhong cried, and tears and sweat were commingled on Hai Rui's face. Team Captain Zhang Wenqi covered his head with a towel, crying by himself in the darkness. This might have been his last chance to participate in the national sports meets, and although his painful right foot had been hard to bear, he insisted on playing a full 40 minutes, personally scoring a game-high 34 points.

But Li Qiuping quickly regained his boldness; the Shanghai men's basketball team after all did manage to create their best achievement in national sports meet history — the best they had done in the past was seventh place — and to win everyone's respect. In the press briefing after the game, Li Qiuping said,

"In the first seven games of the Ninth Sports Meet, we were able to win by big margins, and we easily made it to the finals. I didn't really expect that we would have been able to come as far as we have today. Before tonight's game, I told the players that even without foreign assistance, we have to fight for the championship. The fact is, we did it, and we did very well. This was the break-through point for the league, and our goal has never changed — to win the league championship!"

And Yao Ming, who was constantly surrounded by cameras, had this to say:

"If it had been Wang Zhizhi who had taken the last shot, then this game would have been even more perfect."

Shanghai Sharks team leader Yu Xiaomiao has said that Yao Ming has always gravitated toward a "tumultuous life." He is an idealist who longs to take part in and create classic battles, and even though he lost, he was willing to have lost even more perfectly.

Height Cannot Overcome Irritation

"In 1993, Yao Ming joined the Shanghai municipal team's summer basketball training squad. At that time, he was not yet as tall as the door frame," Li Qiuping analogized. "One year later, when he reported to the youth team, he knocked on my door; when I opened the door and looked, his head was already above the door frame."

When Yao Ming first came to the Shanghai Sports Athletics Technical College's basketball training base, he didn't live in room 305 as he did later on; Li Qiuping arranged for him, Liu

Wei, and Jia Xiaozhong to live together in room 304. Li Qiuping hoped that these three youngsters could later learn to work together to become the core of the Shanghai men's basketball team and be able to know instantly what they needed to do to work together on the court.

But not long afterwards, Yao Ming moved to room 305. "We chased him out," says Liu Wei with a laugh, because Yao Ming was growing too fast and there was just no place for a big bed in the room.

Speaking of Yao Ming's height, the deepest impression on 6'2" Liu Wei was "his big battered head." When they stayed in a hotel, from time to time they would hear Yao Ming cry "Ouch!" — he had bumped his head on the doorframe again.

"Everybody knows Yao Ming's advantage — he's tall. As for his shortcomings — he's tall," Li Qiuping joked. He said that although Yao Ming was usually very careful in the team's quarters and habitually ducked every time he went through a doorway, when they stayed in a hotel on the road, he would often bump his head on the doorframe, and sometimes even set off the fire alarm in the corridor.

When he was very young, Yao Ming realized that he was taller than others his same age — not just a little taller, but nearly a foot taller. He had to pay to ride the bus earlier than the other children, and starting in the fourth grade, he was given the task of washing all of the school's tall windows, something no one else had ever tried.

Wang Jiayin was one year younger than Yao Ming, and the two lived near each other and grew up together. When they were two or three years old, they were about the same height, but afterwards Yao Ming began to "grow by leaps and bounds."

Wang Jiayin complains, "We could all see Yao Ming growing, but our growth was not noticeable."

On one occasion, Wang Jiayin's grandmother joked, "Wang Jiayin, you know, Yao Ming's quite a guy, you two would make a great couple." Wang Jia Yin shook her head and said, "No way! My neck would get so sore having to crane my head to look up at him every day!"

Yao Ming sometimes went to visit his aunt, Yao Zhiying, in the countryside. His aunt took him to play at the elementary school where she worked, and Yao Ming was very active and cheerful, but at the time he still didn't walk too steadily and was always falling down. With a perplexed look on their faces, the teachers would ask Yao Zhiying, "How old is your nephew?"

"See if you can guess." She replied.

"Well, from the size of his head, he's probably about 9 or 10."

At the time, Yao Ming was only 5 years old.

At four years of age, in nursery school, he was 3'9"; at 7, in first grade, he was 4'9"; at 9, in third grade, he was 5'5"; and at 13, in the second year of middle school, he was 6'4". Yao Ming just grew irrepressibly taller like this.

Beginning in 1995, Dr. Wei Guoping of the Medical Office at the Shanghai Sports Athletics Technical College assumed responsibility for Yao Ming's medical supervision and fatigue recovery. Under Dr. Wei's supervision, periodic height measurements were also begun at this time. Dr. Wei says, "Three years after joining the team, Yao Ming had grown 3'9". Even sleeping in bed, he could sense that he was growing."

On the wall next to the door of Dr. Wei's office can be seen some numbers:

March 1995	6' 7"
December 8, 1995	6' 9"
August 22, 1996	7' 1"
January 7, 1997	7' 2"
March 31, 1997	7' 2.6"
June 17, 1997	7' 2.8"
September 1, 1998	7' 3.3"

Next to the door is a scale, and Dr. Wei says: "The scale's height measurement ruler only goes to 6'2", and because we're so primitive here, I used the doorframe to measure Yao Ming's height. I remember very clearly, Yao Ming standing barefooted, pressed up against the doorframe, and I would stand on a bench and take a ruler to measure him."

With regard to Yao Ming's present height, there have been many versions. In the handbook of statistics for Class-A teams in Chinese men's basketball nationwide for 2001-2002, Yao Ming's height is listed as 7'3". So how tall is Yao Ming really? It wasn't until he went to America for a physical examination in May of 2002 that his exact height was definitively given: 7'4".

Wei Guoping says that Yao Ming's true height is between 7'3" and 7'4", but it's probably 7'4" when he gets up in the morning."

After Yao Ming went to the NBA, his big bed in the team's quarters was given to the 6'7" rookie Wang Ligang. This specially-made single bed takes up a lot of floor space with its overall length of 7'8". Before he left, Yao Ming said jokingly to Wang Ligang, "You'd better take good care of my bed. I'm going to take it back from you when I return."

Yao Ming clearly understands that his height is an important bolster of his self-confidence; otherwise, he would not have gone so rapidly from the youth team. "The team didn't have a good center, so that's why they insisted on bringing up us young players."

But when Yao Ming had just begun basketball training, he always felt like he was "lowly" — despite his height, his physique was very deficient, and the preparatory activities in the youth sports school had been very simplistic: do some exercises and then run four laps around the court, and Yao Ming couldn't even run four laps. When he first joined the national team, when he first saw all the "big wrists" like Wang Zhizhi, Mengke Bateer, and also Gong Xiaobin, even though he was taller than they were, he looked up to them.

Naturally, when someone is unexpectedly able to grow to a height of over seven feet, there are bound to be some difficulties.

One time, Yao Ming went out with his teammates Shen Wei and Liu Wei for a stroll in bustling downtown Xu Jia Hui. Not long after getting out of the car, they were surrounded by a noisy crowd. Shen Wei nudged Liu Wei and said, "C'mon, let's get out of here — we don't know him."

"I know I'm taller than everybody else, but there's nothing I can do about it," says Yao Ming. When he was younger, he was always fearful of being in "another category" or "apart from" the other kids, and after he grew up, he had to suffer being a novelty, a spectacle; but contrary to what you might imagine, Yao Ming is very proud of his height.

Everybody calls him "the little giant," but he doesn't like this appellation at all. "Usually, in Shanghai, no matter where I go, people will point at me and say 'Yao Ming, Yao Ming', and that's a very bad feeling. I know that I'm a basketball player who is taller than everybody else, but off the court I don't want to be different from everybody else. So sometimes when I'm just strolling down the street and people point at me, I pretend not to notice, because I have to be able to live my life as a normal person. If someone asks me how tall I am, I tell them: 5'9"."

But in fact, Yao Ming rarely goes out for a stroll.

Yao Ming has quite a few friends, and they are able to see him as an equal, but of course, only psychologically speaking.

"Someone who looks up to me, who regards me as a basketball star and has a photo taken with me or asks for my autograph, could never be real friends with me. What I need is someone who can stand at the same level with me in their heart," Yao Ming says. "To be my friend, the first thing someone has to do is to be unassuming and treat me like a regular person. You know, it's easy for me to treat others like normal people, but it's very difficult for others to be able to treat me like they treat ordinary people."

Emotional adulation often makes Yao Ming feel uncomfortable.

He likes others to speak frankly and without reservation rather than mouthing praise and admiration; he likes others to give him their true opinions and suggestions, not to just venerate and agree with whatever he says; and he likes others to refer to him in an ordinary way.

9. Kingly Airs

Game One: Startling Change

The BaYi Rockets were middle-aged knights-errant who had experienced countless vicious battles; they had ashen faces and curly beards and were covered with scars, yet they were still steadfast and ruthless in battle. The Shanghai Sharks were young swordsmen who had finally attained great results through years of arduous training; they were brightly-garbed raging stallions, eyes blazing like torches, thirsting to attain domination through decisive battle.

Everyone realized that in the 2001-2002 season would come the final showdown at the pinnacle of Chinese basketball that they had been awaiting for seven years.

The Rockets had already won six consecutive overall championships, and the Sharks had made it to the finals for two consecutive years but had left in defeat.

This season, the BaYi team's lineup was in transition following the departure of Wang Zhizhi to the NBA, and they lost seven of 24 regular-season games. But the Sharks, spearheaded by Yao Ming, had lost only one game. After subsequently taking the regular season championship from the Rockets, they made it through the quarterfinals and semi-finals with an undefeated record.

Before the game, the two head coaches went through the formality of shaking hands. Following the tough win over the Jilin team in the semi-finals, Li Qiuping said, "There is only a 2% probability that the Shanghai team will defeat the BaYi team." Ah Dijiang replied, "If you put it that way, then the BaYi team has a 0% hope of victory."

Ah Dijiang, who had taken over from Wang Fei as head coach of the Rockets only four days before the start of the season, was speaking half-jokingly in the face of danger when he said that in the overall playoffs the Shanghai team might win 3 to 0. "If Coach Li lets us play one more game, then we'll play one more game."

April 10, 2002, Ningbo, four great national players in a bloody shark hunt.

This was the first game of the finals, and it was the 65th game hosted by the Rockets in Ningbo. Would the "Ningbo Legend" of the team never having lost at home continue?

As inspiration, Yao Ming grew a scraggly beard on his young face; Liu Yudong shaved his own fierce beard clean off.

The Sharks got off to a fantastic 10-to-2 start, Yao Ming's coverage allowing his teammates to repeatedly break through to the basket and score. Liu Yudong's touch was not bad, hitting three out of three shots, but the score was still 17 to 8.

A smile appeared on Yao Ming's face, a smile that represented an intriguing state of mind. The Shanghai youngsters had unintentionally forgotten that when facing the Rockets they absolutely must not relax even the least, for at any time, any flaw or weak point could prove to be fatal.

Under heavy pressure from the Rockets, the Sharks committed two turnovers, and Mo Ke, Li Nan, and Zhang Jinsong each made three-point shots on the counterattack. The score was tied at 10 all with four minutes remaining in the first period.

Suddenly, the Sharks fell apart. They became upset, tense, and impatient, and their turnovers kept increasing, but the Rockets were as swift as the wind, not letting the opponents have a chance to catch their breath. The score at the close of the first period was 37 to 28, and the Rockets, who had trailed by 9 at one point, had reversed the score to lead by 9.

When the second period began, the Rockets still seemed too vigorous to handle, and at one time they led by 19 points, 62 to 43. They wanted to widen the score to the greatest extent possible.

Li Qiuping resolutely put in David Benoit, an African-American foreign assistance player with NBA experience whom the Sharks had especially brought in to handle "War God" Liu Yudong.

Benoit stuck to Liu Yudong like a shadow, and Liu had no more chance to shoot. The Sharks took the opportunity to gradually close the score, and by the end of the first half, the Rockets were leading by 10 points, 69 to 59.

In the third period, the Sharks found themselves on a roll. With 3 minutes left in the third period, they finally caught up to tie the score, 85 to 85. The Sharks kept on rolling and went on a 12-to-4 run against the Rockets. At the conclusion of this period, the Sharks were leading 97 to 92.

Not long after the start of the fourth period, Mo Ke, who had been guarding Yao Ming, committed his sixth foul and left the game. The Rockets were ice-cold, and the Sharks led 101 to

92. Liu Yudong, who had gone out in the third period because of fatigue, was put back into the lineup, which helped lift the Rockets' morale. They would pass the ball to Liu Yudong, and though Benoit had expended all his strength, Liu Yudong was still his old self, hitting shot after shot, and that almost miraculous shooting stabilized the Rockets' offense.

The offense of the Sharks was completely concentrated in the hands of Yao Ming, who dominated the inside, but two three-pointers from Li Nan and Zhang Jinsong tore open a gap in their defense. The score was now 113 all.

At that moment, Yao Ming was called for a technical foul, and Li Qiuping called that "the turning point of the game." From then on, the Rockets would control the offensive and defensive tempo.

Tied at 115! Tied at 119! Tied at 120! Tied at 122!

The youngsters finally began to grow impatient. Yao Ming had already clearly controlled the inside, but Liu Wei became agitated; he shot from beyond the three-point line, but missed and the Rockets recovered. Then Liu Wei committed a foul, bringing his foul total to six, so he dejectedly went out of the game. After that, Benoit, who had been doing his utmost to guard Liu Yudong, also committed his sixth foul.

Yao Ming penetrated beneath the basket and the opponent fouled, which yielded three big points, and the Sharks were leading 125 to 124. Only 48 seconds remained in the game, so the Sharks still had time for two offensive plays. The ball went to Liu Yudong, and the Sharks triple-teamed him, but Liu found a seam and fiercely passed the ball to Li Nan, who was completely open. With 25 seconds to go, Li Nan, known for his "flying knife" shot, raised his hands and hit a three-pointer. Liu had dealt the death blow to the Sharks.

The Sharks had time for one more offensive play. Foreign-assistance player Steve Hart suddenly broke inside but turned the ball over to the hands of the Rockets. With five seconds remaining on the clock, the Rockets protected the ball and didn't give the Sharks any opportunity to score. Rockets: 127, Sharks: 125.

In this game, Yao Ming made 21 of 21 attempts for an unbelievable shooting percentage of 100%, and he also garnered a CBA-career-high 49 points; that plus his 17 rebounds, six blocked shots, and three steals made him the player with the most outstanding performance. Just as the first half was drawing to a close, Yao Ming scored six points to lead the team in an 8-to-2 run, and that round of offensive plays brought the Shanghai team to within 10 points of the Rockets and laid the foundation for the Shanghai team's use of foreign-assistance players to counterattack in the second half. In the final period, the Sharks scored 28 points, 19 of which were scored by Yao Ming. He was virtually unopposed beneath the basket, and the Rockets ended up losing two of their better players, Mo Ke and Li Ke, to guard him, as both left the game with six fouls.

Liu Yudong did live up to the appellation of "War God." Despite being closely guarded by Benoit during the third and fourth periods, in the entire game he still managed to score 43 points and had 8 rebounds, 5 assists, and 2 steals. After the game, Ah Dijiang also said he was truly a "god." In this game, Liu Yudong's mid-range shooting percentage was 61%, and he made 4 out of 5 three-point shots and 9 out of 10 free throws.

No matter how perilous the situation, Liu Yudong always

kept his spirits, and in the clutch the Rockets always passed the ball to him. After the game was over, Liu Yudong could barely walk.

Li Qiuping said candidly after the game that their defense against the Rockets had been relatively disorganized, they had had too much separation on offense, and their outside shooting percentage was not high. The Rockets had 14 three-point shots but the Sharks only had five.

But although the Sharks, which for a number of years had put themselves in the position of challenger, had lost the first game, their aspirations to win the championship had not suffered in the least.

Li Qiuping's final statement resounded with a thud: "Today the Rockets squeaked by, but in Shanghai we are going to take two games!"

Game Two: Wild and Crazy

April 14, 2002, Shanghai.

"In the first game, we took care of all the little details, the little places that we needed to strengthen. If we can do it all, we can beat them by 10 points!" This was Yao Ming's expectation.

He was full of confidence. The game would be on Sunday, and on Saturday afternoon, he played computer games for three hours by himself in the dormitory in order to relax. In the evening, he chatted on the phone with friends for a long time, not going to bed until 10 o'clock.

The Rockets were also really up for the game, and Ah Dijiang was also very confident: "I hope the Shanghai team's players get a good night's sleep tonight." He was implying that the Rockets were already prepared to take another victory.

Sunday. Not long after the game started, Liu Yudong and Li Nan together scored 11 points, thus putting the Rockets in the lead 11 to 2. But after Li Qiuping called a time out, the Sharks went on a 20-to-4 run to turn the score around and lead 24 to 15 shortly before the end of the first period.

The most difficult time for the Sharks began in the second period when they came up empty on several offensive plays and Yao Ming collected three fouls in struggling for the ball. Also, the Rockets at one point went on a 16-to-7 spurt, and the 10-point advantage that the Sharks had enjoyed when they led 28 to 18 in the first period instantly vanished.

At their closest, the Rockets had caught up to trail by only one point, 30 to 31.

Li Qiuping decisively put Jia Xiaozhong back in to utilize his height on the court while at the same time trying to have Liu Wei control the tempo of the game. At that moment, both teams were not playing at a fast pace, and their scores increased, first one, then the other, moving as if in tandem. Benoit adroitly controlled the star player Liu Yudong, who, hampered by the tight defense, scored only 4 points in the second period. Yao Ming only scored 5 points. The problem was that Yao Ming's movements inside were too frequent, making it difficult for his teammates on the perimeter to decisively pass the ball in to him; the Sharks' scoring relied mainly on mid-range shots and fast breaks.

This situation continued until the third period. In their lineup against the Rockets, the Sharks had always used their pair of foreign-assistance players, Benoit and Hart, in the third period to increase the score going into the fourth period, but this time the Rockets were ready. On the inside, they used Li Ke, who had been playing very well recently, to pair up with Liu Yudong. Li Ke would draw out Yao Ming, and Liu Yudong would complete a mid-range shot near the lane.

However, the Sharks had a method of dealing with this: while tightening up defense of their opponent's passing lanes, Benoit and Hart, cooperated inside and out, and their very dynamic play gradually began to gain momentum on the court. Yao Ming was like a soccer goalie, diving on the floor for the ball, and the experience of the veteran Benoit sparked the entire team's fighting spirit. Even though the Rockets adopted a full-court press defense and offensively went more for long-shot kills, the Sharks still managed to stand firm.

In the third period and the first minutes of the fourth period, these youngsters with soaring fighting spirit went on 15-to-6 and 17-to-9 runs, and with 5:55 left in the game, the Sharks were leading 106 to 83.

With hopes exhausted, Ah Dijiang waved his four national team players, Liu Yudong, Li Nan, Fan Bin, and Zhang Jinsong, out of the game, and Li Qiuping also took Yao Ming out for a rest. Now the game went into "trash time," and was subsequently played out by substitute players for both teams. This had never happened before in the history of match-ups between the Sharks and the Rockets.

After gritting their teeth and making it through the two middle periods, the most difficult part of the game, the Sharks had finally opened a large gap in the last period, flourishing both inside and outside and defeating the Rockets by an unexpectedly large score of 124 to 92.

In this game, Yao Ming played 42 minutes and garnered 26 points, 23 rebounds, 3 assists and 4 steals. Guard Liu Wei contributed 24 points, 10 rebounds, and 5 assists. In addition, five other Shanghai players had double-digit scores.

The Rockets scored only 92 points in the entire game, a record for lowest score since entering the playoffs this season.

In the first game of the finals, when the Rockets defeated the Sharks 127 to 125, Liu Yudong scored 43 points, but in this game he played 30 minutes and scored 27 points. Aside from him, the Rockets' next highest scorer was Li Nan, who contributed 13 points.

In the first game, Li Nan of "flying knife" fame scored 27 points, and Zhang Jinsong, Li Ke, Mo Ke, and Fan Bin contributed 18, 15, 12, and 8 points, respectively; their outstanding performance enabled the Rockets to flourish both inside and outside. Aside from Yao Ming, the Sharks' Liu Wei, Steve Hart, David Benoit, Jia Nan, Zhang Wenqi, and Jia Xiaozhong had tallied 20, 19, 13, 10, and 8 points, respectively, in the prior game.

In the second game, the Rockets' Liu Yudong could not carry the team all by himself, and except for Fan Bin, whose scoring basically didn't change, the scoring of the other main point-makers was sharply reduced. Li Ke and Mo Ke got four points fewer than the first game, Zhang Jinsong scored 8 points fewer, and Li Nan, who had dealt the "coup de grace" in the final seconds of the last game, scored only 13 points.

At the same time as this, the bloodlust had arisen in the Sharks in their home court, and Yao Ming received even more support from his teammates. The scoring of Liu Wei, Benoit, Jia Nan, Zhang Wenqi, and Jia Xiaozhong exploded, and the point totals of the five local mainstays of the Shanghai team as well as the two foreign-assistance players were all in double digits.

After the game, Li Qiuping praised his players: "In this sharp and penetrating offensive attack, low-level turnovers were seldom seen; basically, they never lost the ball, which is a big step forward." He said that the Sharks' performance on offense was just as good as it had been in the first game and went very smoothly. However, the players' offensive desires were too strong and they didn't control the tempo of the game very well and had more turnovers, which led to an extremely low rate of success. "The old players wore themselves out, and in the next game there may be some adjustments as far as they are concerned."

In the game as a whole, the richly experienced Rockets had a total of 19 turnovers, five more than the Sharks. In addition, the Rockets' rebound total was 35, 27 fewer than the Shanghai team. Their free-throw shooting percentage was 57%, which was 13% less than that of the Sharks.

"I said we would win by ten baskets, but I didn't realize how much I underestimated it." Yao Ming said. "Our three-point shots are still so messed up, but by relying on fast breaks and frenzied defense, we still managed to topple them. This is how we beat them in the regular season. And the greatest thing about today is the two giant blocks against Liu Yudong. Even though one was called interference, the other one was just beautiful! Our defense was very successful, and Benoit's guarding of Liu Yudong and the defense of the Shanghai team as a whole was very successful." He joked that the Rockets had been "defendazed."

When Yao Ming played computer games, he usually paid a great deal of attention to efficiency. If he could "kill" the enemy with a single shot, he absolutely would not expend two shots.

In talking about the scene before the final playoffs, Yao Ming very confidently proffered an 'efficiency theory': "If the contest can be concluded 3 to 1, then why should we play on to 3 to 2? The last three games of the final playoff are closer together than the first two, playing one game every other day. This closeness is beneficial to the Sharks but not to the Rockets, who have more older players."

It was also on April 14 that the Yao family happily moved to a new residence.

"Today my parents spent all day moving, but I had to prepare for the game, so I wasn't able to help them. Winning this game was like cutting the ribbon on my new home."

The Yao family originally lived on Twin Peaks Road in the vicinity of Shanghai's 80,000-person gymnasium, and on this day they moved directly across from the Hu Wan Gymnasium. The new house was fairly spacious, about 460 square feet. Yao Ming wasn't sure of the exact size, because he had been busy playing basketball matches, and after renovation of the house was done, he hadn't gone again. "Now it'll be convenient for Mom and Dad to go to games!"

The CBA finals playoff system was three wins out of five games, and on April 17, the Sharks were again the home team. Yao Ming observed:

"The next game is still in Shanghai, and there are only two days separating the last three games; this is the match schedule we want. You don't think the Rockets will fight as hard as they can in the next game? They definitely have two choices: the first is to play against us as hard as they can, and the second is to let the old stalwarts conserve their strength as much as possible and then go back to Ningbo and play really hard in the fourth contest. They want to drag out the match to a fifth game, but it won't be so easy. We've got to destroy their legend of not losing as a home team, but I for one don't believe in that kind of mystical stuff!"

He began to imagine what it would feel like to take the championship in front of the Ningbo spectators at Younger Stadium, the Rockets' home court: "I just can't think what it would really be like, but last year they took the championship at our Hu Wan Gymnasium."

Game Three: A Real Beaut

April 17, Shanghai, a classic slaughter.

In this game, both sides fought with unusual intensity, and the score was very close throughout, the difference never more than seven points.

With 1:54 left in the game, David Benoit made one of two free throws to put the Sharks ahead 124 to 122.

With :57 left in the game, Yao Ming made two of two free throws, making the score 126 to 122.

With :43 left in the game, the Rockets' Zhang Jinsong shot a three-pointer that missed.

With :31 left in the game, Liu Wei made two free throws, and the Sharks led 128 to 122.

With :22 left in the game, Liu Yudong's three-point shot missed, and the Rockets lost their last chance at victory.

With :07 to go, Benoit raised his arms, and the 5,000 spectators in Shanghai's Hu Wan Gymnasium erupted in a cheer never heard before:

"Champions! Champions!"

In the third game of the playoffs, the Sharks defeated the Rockets 129 to 122, and they were closing in on the championship.

"In the past, the Sharks were never as good as the Rockets in taking control of opportunities in clutch situations, but today we scored when we had to and stood up to their onslaughts at key times, " Li Qiuping said.

Although the Rockets had lost and were finding it unusually difficult in defending their title, Ah Dijiang very graciously congratulated the Shanghai team at the post-game press conference. He said that the Rockets had displayed their characteristic skill and tactics in this game and that they had played very colorfully.

From the point of view of the Rockets, this was the best game they had ever played in the final playoffs. They had led their opponents from the beginning of the game all the way through the end of the first half. The Rockets had always been weak in the third period, but this time they played beautifully, not allowing the Sharks to rack up a big lead as their own older players weakened. But in the fourth period, almost every one of the Rockets' shooters was at his mightiest: their three-point percentage was nearly 100% hundred percent, and their shooting percentage in this period was 70%; they held on for dear life, keeping their score close to the Sharks.

In the past, such play on the part of the Rockets would have knocked the opponent over with fright if not defeating them outright. Their unbeatable shooting percentage were what opponents feared most about the Rockets. But this time, in the Hu Wan Gymnasium, the Sharks put on a formidable display. The Rockets would make a three-point shot, and the Sharks would answer in kind; the Rockets would make a two-point basket, and the Sharks would answer by scoring on two free throws. No matter what the opponent did, the Shanghai team never faltered.

To be able to have this kind of achievement is an indication that the Sharks had managed to pass through their toughest barrier — the psychological obstacle. In this game they were not intimidated by the Rockets and did not allow their opponent to "ride roughshod" over them. This was the first time, and because there now was a first time, the Sharks no longer needed to fear the Rockets' "crazy" play. Emotional calm and tenacious fighting spirit are the hallmarks of a mature team. Before, people had seen these things only in the Rockets, but now the Sharks had learned them too.

Yao Ming personally scored 46 points and had 23 rebounds, the most outstanding in the Shanghai team's victory. David Benoit tallied 19 points and 11 rebounds, joining Yao Ming in 'double-doubles'. Zhang Wenqi also contributed 21 points. Altogether, six players on the Shanghai team had double-digit scores.

Old stalwart Liu Yudong played 41 minutes for the Rockets, making 17 of 25 two-point attempts and hitting all 10 of his free throws, collecting the game-high score of 47 points plus 10 rebounds. In the key fourth period, Liu contributed 17 points for the.

Li Nan, who had sunk the game-winning three-point shot for the Rockets in the first playoff game, injured his thigh early on in the second period. But after a short rest, this national team player, whom the fans called "Little Li the flying knife," finished the remainder of the game with a limp. He was on the court for 37 minutes, making 5 of 5 three-pointers and scoring 34 points, a personal best in post-season play.

Perhaps inspired by Li Nan, the Rockets were unusually strong inside and played with extreme tenacity in the face of the Shanghai team with their two foreign-assistance players. In their 32-point loss to the Shanghai team in the second game, the Rockets got 27 fewer rebounds, but in the third game their rebounds were only one fewer than the Sharks.

Before the game, quite a few people conjectured that the Rockets would conserve their strength in the third game, return to their home court at Ningbo and play a life-or-death game four against the Sharks. But Ah Dijiang punctured their speculations.

Before the game, as the court announcer was announcing the Rockets starting lineup, it was discovered that Ah Dijiang had made a change. Li Ke, who had performed well in the two preceding games but who had always come on as a substitute, became a starter, replacing Mo Ke, who had been the Rockets' core center this season.

The result of Ah Dijiang's changing the lineup was not bad. Although Li Ke could not prevent his opponent Yao Ming, who was some 6" taller than he, from scoring beneath the basket, his active defense and tireless running expended Yao Ming's strength. Thus, the power of the Sharks' expanded tight defense centered around Yao Ming waned during the game. At the same time, the Rockets intensified their efforts to grab defensive rebounds and became more patient on offensive plays in the face of pressure.

This plus the stable performance of "War God" Liu Yudong and the revival of Li Nan allowed the Rockets to lead 66 to 62 at the half.

As soon as the second half started, the Sharks sent out Hart and Benoit, just as planned. The Sharks would do their best to string the Rockets along during the first two periods and then in the second half use Hart and Benoit to fight aggressively. But now the Rockets' lineup was quite surprising. Under ordinary circumstances, at the beginning of the second half, the Rockets would send out a core lineup consisting of the four national team players plus Mo Ke. But now, only one of the four national team players, Zhang Jinsong, was on the court, the other four players on the court being the younger players Li Ke, Chen Ke, and Yu Junkai. Were the Rockets about to throw in the towel?

As the game unfolded, Ah Dijiang's intent gradually surfaced. After the second half had been under way for 5 minutes and 40 seconds, people suddenly realized that Hart, Benoit, and Yao Ming were not incurring much advantage against the Rockets' substitute lineup. Going from 62 to 66 and then 75 to 77, the Sharks were unexpectedly able to reduce the difference in score by only two points. Just at this time, Ah Dijiang unfurled his banner, putting the remaining-and now well-rested-national team players back into the game to resume the all-out struggle.

Actually, Ah Dijiang had adopted a similar tactic in the first game of the semi-finals against the Shandong team. When the core lineup did not perform well in the first period, Ah Dijiang sent forth a lineup of young players in the second period. As a result, the young players under the leadership of Li Ke managed to turn the score around and lay down a top performance for the Rockets in winning a key match.

This time, the Rockets' young players again became the dark horse, relying on their copious strength and tenacious defense to hold down the score difference and gain rest time for the older players. When the final showdown began in the fourth period, the Sharks, even with the home court crowd's deafening roar lending assistance, was never able to increase their lead, and with 1:43 left in the game, the Rockets were only two points behind, 122 to 124.

But, the Shanghai team was stronger than the Shandong team, and the Rockets had less luck this time than last time. With 1:04 left in the game, Li Ke failed in a one-on-one attempt against Yao Ming, and with 43 seconds left, Zhang Jinsong's three-point attempt didn't go in. Ah Dijiang's unanticipated lineup change ended up not being able to provide a win for the Rockets as it had in previous games.

Of the Rockets' substitute players, Li Ke was the one with the most outstanding performance. His guarding of Yao Ming in the first game brought him to everyone's attention, as though he had become the Rockets' secret weapon. In the following two games, the Rockets made very judicious use of Li Ke, giving him ample opportunity to display his abilities. His playing time in these three games averaged 21 minutes and his average scoring was nearly 11 points, making his performance that of a core player.

Even Yao Ming said that Li Ke's defense against him was exceptionally good, and even though he couldn't completely prevent him from scoring, he made him expend his strength rapidly. "In the first game, we lost, and though I can't say that Li Ke was the key, nevertheless his guarding me made me extremely tired, and he made quite a contribution toward their win."

Game Four: Overwhelmed

April 19, 2002, Ningbo.

The most perfect contest in the seven years of the CBA: with sudden death, a bag of tricks, Twin Black Wind Goblins, flowers raining from the sky, flying immortals from beyond, mountains of pressure, precision shooting, a sacred dragon shaking its tail, pump fakes and stutter steps, a clean sweep across the board . . . and in the end, facing the wind, a beheading with a single blow.

The final slaughter.

The arena was filled with a thunderous roar, and the spectators were on their feet.

With 2:32 remaining in the game, the score on the court was 115 to 114, the Sharks leading by one point. Li Qiuping called a time out, for in the preceding minute or so, the Sharks' two foreign-assistance players, Steve Hart and David Benoit, had committed two turnovers in a row.

With 2:31 seconds left, the Rockets' 6'8" center Li Ke leapt from the floor and made an "uppity" dunk right over Yao Ming's head, giving the Rockets the lead, 115 to 116.

Benoit then spun and coolly sank a two-pointer, 117 to 116, the Sharks still led by one point.

With 1:37 remaining, Chen Ke, who had gone in for the seriously injured Li Nan, decisively hit a three-pointer, 117 to

119, Rockets.

With 1:11 left, Benoit scored again, 119 even.

Amidst the cacophony, "War God" Liu Yudong shot - but even though he had already made 46 points, but this one did not go in. The spectators gasped as the ball hit the rim and bounced out.

With 32 seconds to go, Yao Ming fought his way under the Rockets' basket, and his long arms reached out to deftly put the ball into the basket, 121 to 119, Sharks.

The Rockets launched another offensive play. After passing the ball several times, Zhang Jinsong, who had drawn two of the opponent's players to guard him, accurately passed the ball to the hands of Liu Yudong, who shot. More than 10,000 eyes watched as the ball soared high through the air in a beautiful arc and fell straight into the basket. Now the Sharks trailed by one point, 121 to 122.

With 7.6 seconds remaining, it looked as though the Rockets' record of never having lost a home game in Ningbo would be extended to 66 games.

Li Qiuping called another time out.

When play resumed, the Sharks threw the ball in bounds. The ball was passed to Yao Ming, who took a mid-range shot and raised both arms ready to cheer, but the ball bounced off the rim and out, and Benoit's follow-up shot also missed. It almost seemed as though the ball had its own will, unwilling to become the culprit responsible for bringing the Ningbo legend to an end.

With 1.1 seconds left, when everyone's hearts were just about ready to stop, an arm suddenly extended in the air and gently poked the ball into the basket.

At that last instant, it was Steve Hart, who had played

unremarkably the entire game, delivering the final score. The Sharks won, 123 to 122.

As the buzzer sounded, Yao Ming spread his long legs and jumped over toward Li Qiuping at the edge of the court, hugging his mentor tightly.

Li Qiuping seemed to be trying very hard to retain his composure, but his fingers were trembling. Though he tried for a whole minute, he was unable to pin a small TV microphone to his lapel.

Elsewhere, the Sharks' Captain Zhang Wenqi was shaking his fists beneath the basket post and yelling at the top of his lungs. Five months before, in the men's basketball finals of the Ninth National Games at Dong Wan in Guangdong, Liu Yudong had slipped past Zhang Wenqi at the last second, and the "War God" had scored the winning three-pointer.

Jia Xiaochong, not a particularly eloquent speaker, yelled over and over, "We are the champions! We are the champions!"

Ah Dijiang, meanwhile, took a long drag on his cigarette. Following the loss, he remained very composed. He smilingly consoled his players, and when later chatting with reporters he often wore a smile. But on his way to the VIP room, he refused to sign autographs for at least three fans. In the VIP room he took three telephone calls, saying only a few words each time, using the imminent start of the press conference as an excuse to hang up. He sat in a cloud of smoke, silent and pensive.

"Today's performance was pretty good, and anybody could have won. That was a tough three-point shot that Liu Yudong made! And Li Nan injured his thigh in the previous game and couldn't recover, but today he toughed it out and was able to play the first half. That shot of Hart's had no chance, Yao Ming is so tall, and if you guard the bottom you can't guard the top. Actually, we shut down Yao Ming, his shots weren't going in, but it took more people to guard him, and Benoit and Hart couldn't make up for that. For us to be able to hold on until now, I think it's been very difficult."

Dragging his injured leg, Liu Yudong walked out of the gymnasium without a backward glance. He had saved the Rockets countless times in the final moments, but his super-long shot at the last second had fallen to the floor far short of the basket.

They had struggled tenaciously to the very last second. Liu Yudong had come on when every game was locked up, and guard Fan Bin had given his all, dragging his left leg, which should have been operated on right away, onto the court. Li Nan, "Little Li the Flying Knife," whose thigh was seriously injured during the third final playoff game, persevered and bore the enormous pain in the fourth game.

The gymnasium was still festooned with the banners and slogans written by the Rockets' fans:

"Tank Hunts Sharks, Don't Waste Any Shots"

"BaYi, Who Can I Love But Thee"

"BaYi, Never Say Bye"

"Heroes Win or Lose, Support BaYi Forever"

"Heroic BaYi, Forge New Glory"

"Heavy Snow Presses on Green Pine, Green Pine Stands Straight and Tall"

"Guard the Ningbo Home Court, Defend the BaYi Dynasty"

"BaYi Warriors, Heroes of Ningbo"

Outside the gymnasium it was raining heavily. At 9:30 p.

m., with championship jackets bearing their logo and the word "CHAMPION" draped over their shoulders, the Sharks, full of vigor, arrived at the awards podium. Team Captain Zhang Wenqi was the first to raise the championship trophy of which the people of Shanghai had long been dreaming, and Yao Ming planted a kiss on the side of the trophy. In this game he had made 56 points and 21 rebounds. But as he tightly grasped the trophy, an anguished look seemed to momentarily cross his face. How much effort had been expended for this moment of joy?

One year earlier, the Sharks had watched the Rockets cut down the basketball nets on their own home court, and now it was their turn to enjoy the spoils of victory. With dazzling gold medals hanging around their necks, Zhang Wenqi made the first cut and Liu Wei followed with the second. Everyone was waving their arms and cheering: Wang Ligang, Jia Xiaozhong, David Benoit, Steve Hart, Jia Nan, Wang Sizhang, Ge Minhui.

Only a couple of pieces of net remained still attached to the rim. One was saved for Yao Ming, and the other was waiting for Li Qiuping.

But Li Qiuping chose this most glorious moment to walk off by himself.

The one person with whom Liu Qiuping most wanted to share this victory was already gone.

As the 42-year-old Liu was moving step by step toward the pinnacle of his career, he lost his love forever. In the afternoon of December 31, 2001, as the entire city of Shanghai prepared to wildly welcome the New Year, Li Qiuping massaged the hand of his wife, Zhang Jue, who was lying in bed at the Ren Ji Hospital. He got up to return to the Sharks' offices to pick up some clothing, and not long after he walked out of the hospital,

Zhang Jue died.

When he heard the news that day, Li Qiuping felt a pain in the pit of his stomach that he had never known. Twice he lost consciousness, and when he awoke, he dashed madly back to the hospital and, bending his large body over, embraced his departed wife, weeping uncontrollably. The two of them had been soul mates for more than a decade, and now, in an instant, they were separated.

Since becoming an adult, Coach Li had almost never wept aloud. After Zhang Jue was found to have stomach cancer in 1998, he lived, for all intents and purposes, in the hospital. When practice and competition grew demanding, Li Qiuping even put a videotape player in his wife's room, and while she slept, he would turn down the volume and study tapes of recent games. As his wife's illness worsened, Li Qiuping's hair grew whiter, and often, in the dead of night, he would embrace Zhang Jue, his tears streaming down uncontrollably. By then his wife, so gravely ill, was no longer able to speak.

In front of others, Li Qiuping seldom if ever shed a tear. On the evening of January 2, 2002, the Sharks hosted the Shanxi SkyCaps, which was Li Qiuping's first game following the loss of his wife. Outside the arena, a bevy of cameras focused on his big, square face, his puffy eyes and the white hair at his temples.

"Coach Li was clearly under much emotional anguish, and he made a great effort to maintain an appearance of strength. At the time, I really wanted to block the cameras, but in fact men don't need to always be like this, men can cry too." said Yao Ming.

But Li Qiuping chose to bear the responsibility and pain by himself. After Zhang Jue was found to have stomach cancer, Li

Qiuping misinformed everyone, and they all thought she had a benign tumor. Even their 11-year-old daughter, Li Mengfei, didn't know the true situation until after her mother had passed away. Li Qiuping fabricated reports about his wife's condition, and he tore the labels off her medicine bottles and put on new ones. Each time his wife asked, "Qiuping, when will I get out of the hospital?" he would smile and say "Soon, very soon." This man, who was known as "Little General" for his cool-headedness and meticulous scheming, bore a smile on his face but a moan in his heart - he was big and tall, imposing, and well-known, but no one could help him.

Yao Ming understood Li Qiuping. Maybe the championship wasn't the most important thing after all. Maybe the most important things were the responsibilities, pain, tears, and affection of the man behind the championship.

At 11 p.m., in the Shanghai TV broadcast booth at Younger Stadium, Yao Ming and Zhang Wenqi sprayed champagne all over the canopy covering the broadcast booth.

At 11:30 p.m., the members of the Sharks and Rockets gathered at Ningbo's "XiangYang Fishing Port" Restaurant. Yao Ming had already shaved off his beard.

At midnight, the celebratory banquet turned into a toasting fest, with everyone raising their glasses in endless toasts, not willing to leave until they were drunk.

Yao Ming usually never drank, but on this night he couldn't stop until he got drunk — it was for the playoffs.

He downed five big glasses in a row.

The first was for the Sharks, naturally.

With the second, he toasted Ah Dijiang. Yao Ming grabbed

him and said, "I take back everything I said about you guys being old. I played 36 games this season, but the six games with you were true contests, and I love to play against you. The Rockets are the greatest." Having spoken, he tilted his head and drained the glass in one gulp.

With the third glass, he toasted Liu Yudong. By then, Yao Ming was already a bit tipsy. Embracing the "War God," he said: "Old Liu, Old Liu, I just hate you to death! No matter how many people guard you, you still play the same!"

With the fourth glass, he toasted Li Nan, who hadn't played much in the fourth game. Yao Ming said to him: "Old Li, when I bumped you that time, it wasn't intentional." With a few drinks under his belt, Yao Ming's face was burning like a fever, but there remained Fan Bin, the "elder brother" of the national team whom Yao Ming respected most.

With the fifth glass, Yao Ming wished Fan Bin a happy birthday: "There's no way I would forget your birthday. When I said that the Rockets were old, you guys got all bent out of shape, but Old Fan, you're the only one who knew what I meant. Now I'm just overcome with emotion. I'm really glad to have been your roomie on the national team for two years."

It rained wildly in Ningbo all night.

None of the Sharks or Rockets slept.

10. Big Yao Journeys West

Earth-Shaking Steps

On the morning of April 29, 2002, Yao Ming departed for Chicago to participate in a trial workout specially arranged for him by the National Basketball Association, thus taking the first step toward joining the world's premier professional basketball league.

Ten days earlier, after the Shanghai Sharks had won the CBA championship in Ningbo, the Sharks' general manager Bai Li announced:

"Today is a day worth celebrating, because the Shanghai team has finally won the long-dreamed-of CBA championship, and now I have brought some more good news for you. The club has already decided that it will not hinder Yao Ming's advancing to the NBA. Yao Ming has opened the door to go to the NBA through his own efforts. He leaves nothing unaccomplished in the CBA, and he ought to go to the NBA to develop further. From today onward, the club will actively discuss with the various NBA teams the specific arrangements for trading Yao Ming, and I guarantee that with regard to the question of Yao Ming going to play in the NBA, the club will not make things difficult for Yao Ming. We hope that soon we will see Yao Ming's outstanding performance on the courts of the NBA."

Yao Songping, the assistant chief of the Shanghai Municipal Sports Bureau, then expressed the following: "On behalf of the citizens of Shanghai, I want to clearly express to everyone that we support Yao Ming's going to play ball in the NBA, and we hope that after Yao Ming arrives on the courts of the NBA he will exemplify Shanghai. If Yao Ming works harder in the NBA, his individual strength will put him among the top ten players in the NBA, and this will be of great significance for Shanghai and for China."

Yao Ming was seemingly already psychologically prepared for all of this, but when it was his turn to speak, he became very emotional: "I originally hoped that I could become the first Chinese player to compete in the NBA, but Big Zhi has gone before me, and Bateer has already set foot in NBA territory, so I will be the third Chinese player to compete in the NBA. I will not abandon my ideals, and I will work just as hard in the NBA."

Li Qiuping no doubt had also made full preparations for Yao Ming's departure from the team. In fact, two years previously he had indicated that, as Yao Ming's skill level increased, the Chinese domestic basketball scene was already unable to satisfy the requirements for his growth — and if Yao Ming left, it would be like the great Shark losing its sharpest tooth:

"As far as any head coach is concerned, Yao Ming is one of those players that, once you use him, you cannot do without him, but the direction for his development lies in the NBA.

Actually, this poses a major contradiction for our team, because on the one hand, we truly cannot do without him, for players like him come along only once in a hundred years, and we don't have any up-and-coming prospects on hand to take his place after he leaves. Without him, the strength of our team overall will greatly depreciate; but if we keep him here on the team, I'm afraid we will be delaying his advancement. So, no matter what, I still hope that he can go to play in the NBA as soon as possible. Even though the ranks of our team will suffer a great loss, we will do our best to make up for it by importing foreign-assistance players, and so on, in the hope that he can carve out a niche for himself in the NBA and win glory for Chinese basketball!"

June, 2002 was Yao Ming's last chance to join the NBA through the draft. NBA regulations state that players participating in the draft cannot exceed 22 years of age, and after September, 2002, Yao Ming would be 22.

Throughout the 2001-2002 CBA season, Yao Ming had become accustomed to seeing the NBA scouts around him.

Visiting VIPs from the NBA were showing up in Shanghai left and right. There was general manager Jerry Krause of the Chicago Bulls, manager Scott Layden of the New York Knicks, managerial assistant Charlie Zhou of the Seattle Supersonics, head of the American Basketball Academy Bruce O'Neil, Memphis Grizzlies head of basketball operations Dick Versace, Toronto Raptors player's personnel manager Jim Keiley, plus the well-known NBA agent Bill Daffey, who represented Wang Zhizhi. Not only did they watch the games at the Sharks' home court, the Hu Wan Gymnasium in Shanghai, they also showed up outside the Sharks' practice court. Those from the NBA had a great deal of praise for the "little giant," describing him as talented and smart, having a broad field of vision, extreme potential, good team spirit, and good passing ability.

Of course, the scouts who had come from America could not avoid "finding fault" with Yao Ming. Some of them said that Yao Ming needed to run more, because in the NBA, the regular season consisted of 82 games, and if you made it to the playoffs you would be playing 119 games, so it was no good if you didn't have good running ability. Some said that Yao Ming was strong enough from the chest down but that he had to strengthen the muscles of his upper extremities. Some were critical enough to notice that when Yao Ming shot, his elbow joints turned a bit outward, and that this would affect his shooting percentage.

They knew full well that before the results of the draft it would not be possible to conclude any sort of agreement, not even a verbal agreement. Nevertheless, they still followed Yao Ming like a flock of ducks. They knew that it would be a major sensation for this incomparably tall, diligent, and intelligent Chinese to appear on the courts of the NBA.

True to expectations, Yao Ming caused an NBA "earthquake" in America.

In his five short days in America, Yao Ming first took his rookie physical examination arranged by the NBA, and put on a "personal show" in front of officials and scouts of the 26 teams. In addition to the "personal show," the NBA also arranged a special session for the Chicago Bulls and the New York Knicks, which made the other teams jealous. The Knicks displayed the most positive attitude toward Yao Ming, and they even invited famous the Chinese movie director Ang Lee to serve as their "persuader."

In one photograph, Yao Ming has a Knicks jersey draped over his shoulders, and almost everybody who is anybody in New York are all gathered together, saying to Yao Ming, "Come to New York, we welcome you."

On May 1, Yao Ming took part in a public training session at Loyola University in Chicago, but he wasn't very satisfied with his own performance.

"Before I went to America, I had gone a week without systematic practice, and when I arrived in Chicago it was already 10 p.m., but then I listened to the planned itinerary for these five days until after 1 a.m., and at 5 a.m. on May 1 I woke up because of the time difference. When I participated in the public workout, for one thing I hadn't adjusted to the time difference, plus before that there was only one hour of warm-up, so less than ten minutes after I got into a practice state and felt that I could take really big breaths, the session was over."

This was a very unusual training session because of the uniqueness of the audience of more than 300, including nearly 70 NBA scouts, coaches, and team officials. The remainder consisted of media from all over the country who had caught wind of the session. This doesn't include the college students and fans that watched from outside the gym. When Yao Ming was shooting baskets, some of them suddenly began shouting, "Jason Williams!" — the Duke University point guard competing to be the number-one draft pick.

The enthusiasm of the American press for Yao Ming could be seen at this workout session. Some media reports said that hopefully Yao Ming "could become a center to match up against Shaquille O'Neal" — which made Yao Ming feel that he was bearing a heavy burden indeed.

On May 2, Yao Ming underwent a basic physical examination, which included the cardiovascular system, muscular and skeletal system, physical ability, and special basketball attributes. Originally, the examination was expected to be very simple, but it ended up taking the entire day, and the seriousness of the Americans made him really experience a bit of NBA professionalism.

"Let's talk about the X-rays." He said. "Originally, I thought they would just take maybe three or four, at least that's what they do back home. Guess how many they ended up taking? 32!"

There were three MRI scans; twice on the knee joints, which is normal; what was unexpected was that Yao Ming casually mentioned that the hearing in his left ear had been affected by a childhood illness, and another MRI was performed on his left ear. Yao Ming, who was by now really tired, had been expecting to use a few hours to take a nap, but he didn't get the chance with the MRI machine humming next to his ear.

Setbacks on the Road to Happiness

Right around the time that Yao Ming was about to go to America to take part in the NBA trial workout, both domestic and foreign Chinese media began to "reveal" two documents recently produced by the National Sports Bureau's Basketball Management Center, "Management Methods for Basketball Sports Agents" and "Methods of Managing Foreign Trades of Basketball Athletes," which were issued in draft form on April 5 and in final form on April 10. Public opinion was focused upon the distribution of profits of athletes playing abroad in "Methods of Managing Foreign Trades of Basketball Athletes."

"Methods for Managing Foreign Trades of Basketball Athletes" quoted the National Sports Bureau's "Information Bulletin Regarding Questions Pertaining to Regularization of Sports Management Center Operations," part five, paragraph four:

"The prize money of national team players who participate in competitions with major prizes and various commercialized matches should be distributed according to the following principle, giving consideration to the benefit of all parties, in accordance with the relevant methods of the National Sports Bureau: 50% to the athlete, coach and other contributing personnel, 30% to the prize fund or development fund of the particular sports association, 10% to the province (municipality, district) of the athlete and coach, and 10% to the General Sports Bureau."

"Provisional Methods for Managing Foreign Trades of Basketball Athletes" also stipulated:

"Paragraph Two: Transfer of a domestically registered player to a club outside the country (territory) requires the tripartite agreement of the player, the player's club (sports team), and the local sports management department, and the club (sports team) and the basketball sports agent must apply to the Chinese Basketball Association. The Chinese Basketball Association will handle the examination and approval procedures.

"Paragraph Ten: Any contract agreement between a basketball club (sports team), basketball agent and a player signed with a foreign club is invalid if it has not undergone examination and approval by the Chinese Basketball Association.

"Paragraph Twelve: Besides conforming with Paragraph Two, any current national team player leaving the country to play ball must sign an agreement with the Basketball Association covering the following content in addition to Paragraph Eleven: (1) unconditional subordination to the interests of the State; (2) participation in national team practice and competition as scheduled and in accordance with requirements; (3) positive demeanor and exemplary observance of rules while serving on the national team - negative behavior or the incurring of any disciplinary punishment will nullify any agreement signed with foreign parties; (4) periodic reporting to the Chinese Basketball Association of conditions abroad with regard to living, training, competition, and infirmity — should infirmity occur, the Chinese Basketball Association may, in view of the circumstances, request the athlete to timely return home to recuperate; (5) the foreign party must guarantee the proper rights and dignity of the Chinese player; (6) the player's club and the player himself may not impugn the dignity of China in word or deed; (7) the player must keep secret such information as skills and tactics of the national team.

"Paragraph Fourteen: Players traded abroad (including players who are foreign nationals) should submit a one-time trade processing fee to the Chinese Basketball Association. Chinese players will submit a fee of RMB$1,000.

"Paragraph Fifteen: Athletes will not fulfill any contract detrimental to the interests of China, and, depending upon circumstances, the Chinese Basketball Association will exact the following penalties: (1) monetary fine; (2) suspension of play in domestic matches from a period of one year up to lifelong suspension; (3) request foreign basketball associations and sports organizations to administer corresponding penalties; (4) for national team members, expulsion from the national team and abrogation of all agreements with foreign parties.

"Paragraph Eighteen: These measures are effective as of April 10, 2002."

Just as Yao Ming was about to become the third Chinese player to make the journey to the NBA, this management method was promulgated. There was a public outcry: Was this document specifically directed at Yao Ming?

Xu Minfeng, head of the Basketball Management Center

office and news spokesperson, indicated that the timing was co-incidental and that it was not directed at Yao Ming. Xu said by way of introduction that these two management methods had earlier been considered for release during the prior season, but that some time had been required to draft them, and at the same time it had been necessary to solicit the opinions of the various CBA clubs. He remained very sanguine about Yao Ming's prospects for joining the NBA.

"It is no more than pure coincidence, and we did not have the intention of taking aim at any particular player," the National Sports Bureau's Basketball Management Center formally declared its position on April 25, "and we fully support Yao Ming's going to the NBA to play ball."

Hu Jiashi, assistant to the head of the Basketball Management Center, said that with regard to Yao Ming's going to the NBA to participate in the draft, the Basketball Management Center had maintained a supportive attitude throughout. As for the "Management Methods for Basketball Sports Agents" and "Methods of Managing Foreign Trades of Basketball Athletes," "Wang Zhizhi and Mengke Bateer, who previously went to the NBA to play ball, were able to do so only after following these procedures, and Yao Ming will not be an exception. Moreover, with regard to submission of wages and prize money, the National Sports Bureau and the Basketball Management Center had these regulations before; they are not aimed at Yao Ming. In fact, the Basketball Management Center began to study the institution of regulations in this area last year, but due to weighing various aspects and repeated consideration, they were only recently formally announced. In addition, these two provisions encompass the various rights and duties of players going abroad to play ball, and it should be said that they embody the interests of all parties. We were not intending that they be directed against Yao Ming." Regulating the distribution percentages in this manner was also carried out completely in accordance with the pertinent regulations of the National Sports Bureau. In October of the previous year another document had been issued requiring implementation strictly according to the rules as of 1997. In the view of the Basketball Management Center, this kind of "distribution" was "in keeping with the realities of China's competitive sports system." For no matter whether it be Yao Ming or Wang Zhizhi and Mengke Bateer who had already gone to the NBA, all were under the "nationwide system" and had been nurtured by the State, which was completely different from the situation of players abroad, whose development was through personal investment.

At the same time, Hu indicated that the documents now put forth by Basketball Management Center, in addition to these "Methods," were also related to sports agents' management methods. The reason for so doing was mainly because in the last two years there were more domestic players going abroad and it was necessary to come out with relevant standards.

Xin Lancheng, head of the Basketball Management Center and secretary-general of the Chinese Basketball Association, later unequivocally indicated that the Chinese Basketball Association supported Yao Ming in going to the NBA to play ball, and he hoped that the media would not make a fuss over the question of his submitting part of his income according to regulations. "The Chinese Basketball Association has the means to bring this matter to a good resolution."

The Number One Draft Pick

"The Houston Rockets' first pick: Yao Ming!"

On June 27, 2002, at 7:36am Beijing time, through a small, special television amplifier the size of a box of tea, Yao Ming heard from thousands of miles away the voice of NBA Commissioner David Stern in New York's Madison Square Garden.

At that instant, Yao Ming laughed, and grinned, and his eyes closed tightly.

This was the most exceptional draft selection in NBA history, when a bunch of earnest young talents clad in suits and leather shoes gathered round Stern like stars surrounding the moon, the real star was not even present. He was coiled up in a small, narrow room, casually dressed in a T-shirt, wearing a hat that was too small, his eyes still filled with sleep, and with a stubborn cowlick on the back of his head. But he was the first pick, the first first-pick rookie in NBA history without a background in American basketball.

The place where he was, a makeshift broadcast booth less than 80 square feet in size, was actually the apartment of a foreign reporter outside the Jian Guo Gate in Beijing. Because he had to participate in the Chinese men's basketball group training, there was no way Yao Ming could go to New York to attend the draft convention. The TNT cable network, which owned the direct-broadcast rights for this draft, had set up a branch conference room for Yao Ming. Although they couldn't see images from the draft conference, they could directly hear the voice of David Stern announcing Yao Ming's selection.

Yao Ming arrived at 6:45 a.m. He was wearing a short-sleeved Chinese team T-shirt and black training pants, and when he bent over to enter the door, behind him was Head Coach Wang Fei of the Chinese national team. The two men's eyes were slightly red, and it was evident that they were not accustomed to getting up so early.

Ten minutes later, Yao Ming's parents, Yao Zhiyuan and Fang Fengdi, arrived. Because their plane was a bit late, they did not arrive in Beijing until after one o'clock in the morning on the 27th. Though they had not slept for the entire night, the two were still fresh and spirited. They were invited into a broadcast booth which had been a bedroom converted for use as an office and into which a staggering array of broadcasting equipment, lights and reflectors, video cameras, and microphones had been placed, filling the room entirely. Facing the camera were four chairs, which were pushed very close together due to lack of space.

With the combined presence of Yao Ming, Yao Zhiyuan, Fang Fengdi, and Wang Fei, this room was simply too small. Xinhua News Agency reporter Xu Jicheng served as Yao Ming's translator. Also present were TNT network executives, along with technician Zhang Xiuqing of the Hong Kong NBA Corporation.

Five minutes before Stern's announcement, Zhang Xiuqing took out five Houston Rockets caps and gave one cap to each person. Rookies putting their caps on was a traditional event in the draft, for when you put the cap on, it signified that you were a member of that team; usually, you would put on the cap and go up onto the stage after Stern tore open the envelope and read your name. But with a wide grin, Yao Ming planted the cap firmly on his head, just like he was already a "Rocket."

Finally, the tiny amplifier transmitted the sound of Stern's voice, short and clear.

The broadcast director and moderator of the TNT television company and the technician of the NBA's Asian corporation were the first to cheer.

But the three members of the Yao family hid their happiness in their hearts and didn't jump for joy as the Americans had imagined. They hugged one another, and Yao Ming and his parents applauded happily only at the prompting of the others; then they began to high-five one another in celebration.

Zhang Xiuqing had Yao Ming hurriedly put on his cap, and Yao Ming tried to pull it down firmly on his head, but it wouldn't go on. He pulled down hard, but when he let go, the cap shifted up again, perched on the top of his head, so Yao Ming gave up and left it alone.

The new first pick earnestly expressed his feelings to the camera: "There will be many challenges in the NBA, and many difficulties. I think the most important thing is how to go there and learn, so that our country's level in basketball can be raised even further."

After being selected, Yao Ming had five minutes for interviews, the images being directly transmitted to the draft conference in New York. After routinely answering two questions, everyone took a short break. Then Yao Ming grew more animated. Holding the Rockets cap, he said,

"I've played against the "Rockets" for several years, and I never thought that I'd become a Rocket." Wang Fei, who was next to him, also laughed.

Then Yao Ming took questions from the Houston media,

and when a reporter asked him which NBA team he wanted to play against, Yao Ming decisively said, the Lakers. Which player did he most want to play against? Yao Ming said, the Lakers' best center, but he didn't mention O'Neal by name.

When a Houston reporter asked Yao Ming to use English to say hello to his new city and new fans, Yao Ming used English very fluently to say:

"I am very happy to join the Houston Rockets. Hi! Houston, I'm coming."

The reporters on the other side of the ocean asked Yao Ming to hold the microphone closer and say it again, as they wanted to record these words so that every Houston fan could hear them. This time, Yao Ming flashed a smile:

"OK, I'll say it again. I AM VERY HAPPY TO JOIN THE HOUSTON ROCKETS. HI, HOUSTON, I'M COMING."

After that, Yao Ming fell into the clutch of reporters waiting outside the makeshift studio. Though it was the time of the Korean-Japanese World Cup, there was still a gaggle of reporters who had showed up on their own. Even when he went to the bathroom, they wouldn't let him alone. The crowd of video cameras shone their lights on the bathroom door, and when he came out, the flash cameras went off like a burst of machine-gun fire. When he went from one room to another, no matter where it was, he had to stop and answer a host of questions.

Just then, Yao Ming's cell phone rang. It was Rockets Head Coach Tomjanovich making the first call of the day for Yao Ming. Holding his phone, he wanted to get away from the reporters, so he ran into the room he had been in first, not realizing that a large group of reporters had wormed their way in from outside, and he was surrounded by banks of video cameras — by then, the "cordon" at the door could no longer hold them out. With precise pronunciation, Yao Ming said, ". . . That's right, here is very far away from New York." For the next four and a half minutes, Yao Ming used simple English to converse with Tomjanovich, but most of the time he was listening. After the phone call was finished, he said that he was able to understand "50 to 60 percent" of Tomjanovich's English.

Fang Fengdi and Yao Zhiyuan stood in the passageway outside the room. Their expressions were ordinary, as though nothing wonderful had happened to their son this day.

Waving Goodbye and Saying Hello

"Yesterday in San Francisco somebody asked me, 'Can I borrow your map? I live in Houston.' I told him that I live in Houston too, but that I've never been there before." —Yao Ming

On July 25, 2002, representatives from the Houston Rockets flew to Shanghai and opened talks with the Sharks basketball club pertaining to Yao Ming's joining the NBA. For Yao Ming to go to the NBA, the Sharks demanded "ten major gifts" of Houston all at once: (1) help in finding two high-level foreign-assistance players; (2) closed group training for the Sharks in Houston for one month; (3) periodic training of Sharks' management and coaching staff at the Houston Rockets' facilities; (4) the Rockets coming to Shanghai for an exhibition game; (5) Rockets' stars coming to Shanghai to take part in publicity events; (6) joint establishment of a basketball school by the Rockets and the Sharks; (7) Rockets provide coaching assistance to the Sharks; (8) obtain funding from Rockets' sponsors to establish a training facility in Shanghai; (9) Rockets to pay compensation of US$350,000; and (10) the National Basketball Association establish a special policy for the city of Shanghai with regard to television broadcasts.

The Sharks basketball club had a plethora of reasons: Yao Ming was the "Michael Jordan" of the team, and was it easy to nurture a "Jordan?" With Yao Ming gone, every aspect of the Sharks' achievement, box office, sponsorship, would be greatly affected; thus, ten conditions for compensation were not at all excessive in their view. In fact, many of the conditions consisted of "verbal" agreements which had been made early on during initial negotiations.

But the Houston Rockets took a different view. Michael Goldberg, their attorney who had come to Shanghai, felt that according to NBA regulations, aside from the payment of trade compensation fees, NBA teams were not allowed to develop other economic relationship with foreign teams.

He cited an example: the Minnesota Timberwolves team secretly signed a "sub-rosa" contract with a player, and when this was discovered, the Timberwolves were heavily fined by the NBA and lost their first-round draft-choice rights for five years.

Goldberg also made a leisurely attempt to sell the notion that if Yao Ming went to play in the NBA, the Sharks basketball club would in fact be making a major sacrifice, but that this would lead to the promotion of Chinese basketball in general.

The Sharks organization were disappointed with Goldberg's seeming role as "matchmaker" and made it widely known that they wanted to speak directly with the NBA, and it seemed that Goldberg's trip to Shanghai might turn out to be in vain. Everyone expected that he would only be able to convey the Sharks' conditions back to America, and that the two parties would subsequently conclude a compensation agreement via facsimile — thus, for the time being, the matter of Yao Ming was unresolved.

However, on the evening of the 27th, when Goldberg returned from a day-long outing in Shanghai, he was happy to see that the contract document had already been signed.

By signing his name, Yao Ming freed himself.

The final signing of the contract led to a great deal of speculation, but one thing certain is that the Sharks basketball club made enormous concessions, and Goldberg made verbal promises to the Sharks on behalf of the Houston Rockets.

As to whether these verbal promises were made perfunctorily in the urgency of the moment or whether they are true and honest promises, only time will tell. However, for a basketball market as enormous as China, a single gift may be repaid many times over, and the NBA, in its dark and mysterious ways, doubtless understands this very well.

Yao Ming chose to follow again a road to growth, and to say goodbye to his home, at least for the present.

On October 19, with memories of the past appearing one after another before his eyes, and filled with emotion and some sadness, he set forth on his journey.

First he returned to the Mei Long training base at the Shanghai Physical Education and Sports Academy, where he had spent the most important part of his growth.

He dropped in everywhere, and the gang all laughed and

joked with him as before, wanting him to "invite them to an abalone dinner." Yao Ming laughingly replied, "Wait till the abalone grows a little bigger and then I'll invite you."

The brass placard bearing his name was still on the door of room 305, the stuffed teddy bear hanging on the wardrobe was still there, and the bedding was neatly arranged, almost as though he had still been living there the day before. He asked all the reporters to leave the room, staying behind by himself to silently remember all the trials and hardships of the past nine years.

After returning from his walk down memory lane, Yao Ming took part in the going-away party the academy had arranged for him. "Success to Yao Ming in joining the NBA; may Yao Ming return after succeeding in his endeavors," read a large banner hung right in the middle of the conference room.

The words of advice of Ye Beilun, party committee secretary of the Shanghai Physical Education and Sports Academy, were "come home to visit often," and she asked Yao Ming, "Is there anything that you haven't had time to take with you?" Yao Ming laughingly replied, "My bed." Ye Beilun said, "We'll save this bed for you forever."

He had endless words for his mentor, Li Qiuping. Li gave him a gift, and when a reporter asked what it was, he said with a laugh, "What can we coaches afford to give? As coaches, we have succeeded if we can send him out."

What he gave to his disciple was a wristwatch infused with eight years of friendship between teacher and pupil.

In the afternoon, Yao Ming arrived at the Gao An Road First Elementary School, and his primary school teacher, Gong Lingzhen, was waiting for him.

Yao Ming gave his teacher a bouquet of fresh flowers, and

Gong Lingzhen was deeply moved: "I have taught for 37 years, and to be able to have educated a student like Yao Ming really makes me very happy."

Having returned to his alma mater, Yao Ming still had a very important mission, which was to film a TV documentary with Shanghai Television's sports channel depicting his experiences while growing up. The filming location was set up in the basketball gym at the Gao An Road First Elementary School, and here Yao Ming encountered his first coach, Li Zhangmin. When master and pupil met, there was endless conversation, but the time allotted to them was short.

Qian Jiacheng, the young actor who plays Yao Ming as a youngster in the documentary, turned out to be a student of Coach Li Zhangmin. He had just graduated from the Gao An Road First Elementary School, and in all respects he is considered to be Yao Ming's "junior fellow apprentice." Even more unusual is that Qian Jiacheng is already 6', which is taller than Yao Ming was at that age. Who knows whether he might become another "little giant?"

After leaving his alma mater, Yao Ming went back to his old residence on Kang Ping Road, where he spent his childhood.

When he had just walked into the courtyard downstairs, he hollered out, "How did this courtyard get so small?"

He had grown up, but the courtyard was as it had been in his childhood.

As evening approached, Shanghai Mayor Chen Liangyu personally met with Yao Ming at the Heng Shan Hotel. Chen said to Yao Ming, "You are about to go to America to play ball, and we are all very happy; Shanghai is willing to make the sacrifice for the cause of Chinese basketball. Your growth is the result of

the concern of and nurturing by the people, and it is also inseparable from your own efforts. In the future, all of us will continue to be concerned for you, and we will applaud every bit of
good news about you from over there!"

Yao Ming said, "I will firmly remember everyone's trust in
me, and I will carry the hopes of the people of China in my
heart as a motivation to progress."

He was really leaving.

In the early morning of October 20, 2002, at the international entrance at Shanghai's Hong Qiao Airport, Yao Ming
turned his head around and looked backwards for the third time,
waving vigorously.

He was waving goodbye to Shanghai, the homeland in which
he had been born and raised for 23 years.

Through the window of Air China flight 929 from Shanghai to San Francisco, he could see the boundless ocean.

The whole world was focused on the other side of that great
ocean, for a Chinese was about to arrive.

Conclusion

Looking back over his first season with the NBA, Yao Ming recalled:

"Everything is difficult at the beginning. At that time, I felt like a stranger in the basketball circle, not like in the past. I had great pressure which was like an invisible wall falling onto me, making me panic in complete darkness."

For Yao Ming, his first season was meant to get himself adapted to his new environment. He lives in a magnificent house in an exclusive area of Houston, and enjoys his mother's home-cooked meals. "In my first season in the NBA, I felt like I was sitting on a roller coaster, up and down, up and down. But the experience was very precious for me. If I were not in the NBA, it would take years for me to accumulate these experiences. I have gained so much in the year, thanks to the help from my colleagues and fans."

"I will never forget my first match in the NBA, against the Indiana Pacers on October 31, 2002. When I went through the long passage on to the court, I felt the atmosphere made me numb. I was really very nervous."

Yao Ming did not score in his first game and was very frustrated. His teammate, Steve Francis said, "It has passed. There are eighty more matches." Yao Ming's former coach and friends in Shanghai also told him: "It's all right. You have a long way to go." His mother, Fang Fengdi said nothing about the match to him at home. But Yao felt the warmth of his family which always gives him confidence.

Fighting SARS and Looking Ahead

Yao Ming returned to Shanghai on April 20, 2003, to train with the Chinese national team for the Asian Basketball Championship.

"I will taste all the breakfast snacks in Shanghai this time," said Yao Ming. He was very excited when he was back to his hometown, and was eager to meet with family and friends. "I will readjust myself in Shanghai since I have not had enough sleep for quite a long time." He said.

Yao Ming returned to China at a critical time, during the worst months of the SARS (Severe Acute Respiratory Syndrome) epidemic. When Yao Ming stepped off the plane in his white Nike jacket, the first group of people who came to meet him were not reporters but doctors. Yao Ming was seated and his temperature was taken with the latest heat-sensing medical equipment. Yao Ming could not believe it.

Like other cities in China, Shanghai had fallen under the

shadow of SARS, a deadly infectious virus about which we still know very little. Many foreigners had already left China; but why did Yao Ming choose this time to come back from his house in the U.S.? Yao Ming merely smiled and said: "It's my home."

In his first season, he has become a key player in the Houston Rockets organization, and is well-known in the U.S. where he now has legions of devoted fans. Whereas other NBA players took vacation during the off-season, Yao Ming was coming back to China to play ball.

Well before Yao Ming returned to Shanghai in the Spring of 2003, he was already on the list of the Chinese national team. Here, he would prepare for the Asian Basketball Championship. The winning team would automatically advance to the 2004 Olympic Games in Athens.

In May, Yao Ming appeared at the Shanghai Military Medical College, wishing the Shanghai special medical team well as they prepared to travel to Beijing and combat the deadliest concentration of SARS cases in China. This was Yao Ming's first public appearance in China after returning from the U.S.

"I felt the atmosphere a bit stiff because of SARS when I arrived from the U.S." He said. "Now I realize that with a common effort, we can overcome any difficulties no matter how big they are."

Ever since he returned to China, Yao Ming has become very concerned about the prevention of SARS and was greatly moved by the devotion of the medical workers. He gave autographed basketballs to the members of Shanghai's medial team. He also joked, "I am so tall, so I will not easily get SARS."

In May, 2003, Yao Ming's official Chinese website (http://yaoming.net/china) was officially launched.

At the opening ceremony, Yao Ming said, "Everybody knows that I am an internet fan. Now I have my own website and hope that it will shorten the distance between myself and others."

During the website opening ceremony, Yao Ming held a press conference. It was the first time he was interviewed by the Chinese media since he returned from the U.S. that spring. He was still himself — intelligent, humorous, and emotional.

Why did you choose this time to come back when SARS is not fully controlled? You may stay in the U.S. until the gathering of the Chinese national team. Is this a commercial consideration?

No commercial consideration. This is not a difficult decision to make. I am just returning home.

What is your feeling about SARS?

Frankly I was a bit worried before I came back, but when I see the situation I am feeling much more confident. People are taught how to prevent and control SARS. I am sure that SARS will soon be under control.

What impressed you the most?

The medical workers who are fighting SARS. They put the safety of others above their own, and work in the most dangerous places. They are the ones to be respected.

How did you get the idea to initiate and participate in the "Combating SARS" TV program?

As a Chinese, one can never forget his own country, his home town. I cannot sit idle when everybody is fighting SARS. I wish that I will do my best and help more patients get more help, and help the medical workers get more protection. Protecting them is actually protecting ourselves. In the program, I want to increase the confidence of the audience in combating SARS.

What kind of program is it?

We will conduct interviews and have some special programs. We will accept fundraising donations via telephone. We will also invite some sports stars to talk to the audience. You will be surprised, but I cannot tell you more now.

Why did you choose this time to launch your website?

I launched my website at this critical time in order to collect donations for the medical workers who are fighting SARS, and for the China Red Cross and other medical institutions. To make my contribution, I chose this time to launch my website. Thanks to all of you who attended the opening ceremony. Here we do not have red ribbon, but only a telephone line. I hope you won't cut it!

Do you feel safe when you come out to take part in public events?

My parents are also worried about me. They asked me not to go out too often. But I feel quite safe. I may have a chance to meet with friends and have a chat. This safety is given by the medical workers. I wish more people will enjoy a happy and free life like I do.

How do you protect yourself from SARS?

I am tall. I inhale more fresh air than others, so it's not easy for me to get SARS. This is just like getting a higher point during warfare. I am joking! I wash hands almost every hour, plus I eat healthy food. During this period I have had fewer physical training sessions, but will do more soon. Everyone wants to be healthy. My method is to have healthy food and exercise. Nowadays, young people have more pressure, but you have to pay more attention to health. Regular exercise and outdoor activities will ensure enough energy and health. During this period, I suggest you continue exercising in a safe environment. Now, some people are too scared of SARS. Don't live in the shadow of SARS everyday. Anyway, we have to continue our life.

On May 10, Yao Ming's "open letter" was published in newspapers around Shanghai:

Ladies and Gentlemen:

On April 26, I ended my first season of NBA matches and flew to Shanghai Pudong airport, where I experienced an unexpected health check. The masked medical worker told me that Shanghai, my hometown, and China, my home country, are experiencing a sudden and smokeless war. During this war, no one can stay away from it no matter whether you are rich or poor, famous or not.

Up to now, there are 4,805 people who have been infected with SARS, among whom 230 have died.

The war is an arduous and protracted war, because before the vaccine and other effective medicines are invented, the best way is to stop the spread of the virus. However, the medical workers working at the front lines have left their families and take the risk to enter the zone of separation to save patients. At present, 900 of them have been infected and five have died. The youngest doctor, Li Xiaohong, died at the age of 28.

The war is a scientific war. Whether we can finally defeat SARS all depends on the breakthroughs in science. Scientists in China and in the rest of the world are working day and night to combat the unknown virus, winning time and saving lives.

To fight the war we have closed theatres and cinemas and postponed sports matches. But this will not shake our resolution and courage to win the final victory. We are sure that the final victory will be ours.

I think that we should do our best to thank the medical workers who have been sick or who have lost their lives, to support the scientists who are working hard, and to encourage the public to discard panic and establish confidence. All these efforts shall be made to arouse the whole society to defeat SARS, the common enemy of mankind. On Sunday, May 11, I will participate with Shanghai TV, together with other Chinese and foreign media, to launch a live program broadcast throughout the country. During the live broadcast, donations through telephone calls and the internet will be accepted. Through the China Red Cross and in the name of all the medical workers who have lost their lives, all the money will be used for the prevention of SARS for medical workers, and for further scientific research into halting SARS.

At the same time, through the media, we will call on everybody to establish our shared confidence in defeating SARS. Taking part in and supporting combat against the SARS is the obligation of every citizen. As a member of the global village, your help is not to be ignored and is very important to us. We hope that you will make a donation, showing your concern and support for the medical workers and scientists. At the same time, your action will also help us establish our confidence to overcome the difficulties ahead. Your action will win the gratitude and respect from the whole country. I'm looking forward to your participation and support.

Sincerely,

Yao Ming
A Chinese citizen

Beginning at 5pm on May 11, 2003, the Sports Channel of Shanghai TV and Shanghai Satellite TV jointly hosted a three-hour live telethon: "Super Stars Combating SARS."

Yao Ming spoke: "This society belongs to everyone. We all should care about our society. If there is any difficulty, we will shoulder it together." The live broadcast generated over U.S. $280,000, which was transferred to the China Red Cross.

David Stern, Commissioner of the NBA, Yao's teammate Steve Francis, tennis star Andre Agassi, and golf star Tiger Woods all appeared on screen. Former U.S. president Bill Clinton wrote a letter which was read on air:

"No matter where you are, in China or in the United States, I call on everyone to make your contribution to protect the medical workers from the threat of SARS. I want to thank Yao Ming for his support and also thank him for his hosting tonight's program."

Sincerely yours,

Your friend and basketball fan,
Bill Clinton

Many other sports stars, movie stars, and performing artists from China and Hong Kong participated in the program. All donated money or items to be auctioned off as fundraisers for the event. Yao Ming donated one of his national team jerseys, shoes, and autographed basketball. It was later learned that he had personally given US$60,000.

At the end of the program, Yao Ming found that he could not raise his arm, because he had done so many autographs that night. He ended the telethon with the following words: "Let us link our hearts together to form a great wall of health; let us join our hands together to form a sea of hope." He touched many that night.

On October 1, 2003, Yao Ming joined the Chinese national team as they defeated the defending champions, South Korea, 106 to 96 to take the Asian men's basketball championship in the northern Chinese city of Harbin. Not surprisingly, Yao Ming was voted MVP of the tournament, scoring 30 points in the final championship game. With this win, China automatically advances to the 2004 Olympic Games in Athens.

Yao Ming now begins his 2nd season in the NBA. Hopefully, we've all learned a bit more about him and will continue to watch him in the years ahead.

Afterword

This book was written very much by chance. At the end of 2000, in order to complete the drafts of a large quantity of sports articles during a time when there weren't many sports competitions, I made an arrangement with my mentors in the sports department of the Xinhua (New China) News Agency to begin gathering materials for a long news report, "Yao Ming's Journey," about Yao Ming's growing up.

Gathering news is naturally hard work, but after the serialized publication of this group of reports began on January 5, 2001, they were well received, and were serially published by numerous Chinese media organizations nationwide. Simultaneously, some book publishers contacted me at one time or another, and I then realized that everybody was very interested in how Yao Ming grew up. I then collaborated with the Shanghai University of Finance and Economics Press because, on the one hand, Yao Ming is truly a big and tall representative of the heroes of modern China — Shanghai in particular, and on the other hand, Press Director Wang Lianhe encouraged me to write the book.

Shifting from writing articles to writing a book, I felt enormous pressure. I had never thought that my first book would be about a sports star. A few years ago, there was a publisher in southern China that invited me to write a biography of Korean soccer coach Cha Bun Keun, and some preparations were made. But then, due to my laziness, nothing came of it. This time, I buckled up and accepted the task, but an even greater reason was that I was personally interested in the process of Yao Ming's growing up: his personal story in a way perhaps epitomizes the profound changes of China over these last twenty years.

To inform the reader about the real Yao Ming is not an easy task. In the eyes of ten different people there are ten different Yao Mings; yet they all have one point in common — Yao Ming was a good child. I can but do my utmost to write about a Yao Ming as close to the real Yao Ming as possible.

I must thank a great many people for making it possible to complete this book in such a short time, including Yu Xiaomiao, Li Qiuping, and Liu Wei of the Shanghai Sharks Basketball Club, Wang Zhongguang, Yan Zijian, Wang Jumei, Yao Ming's aunt, Yao Zhiying, Yao Ming's teacher, Gong Lingzhen, and his first coach, Li Zhangmin, my Xinhua News Agency colleagues Xu Jicheng, Wang Jingyu, Shan Lei, Pan Yi, and others too numerous to mention.

Many of my fellow journalists have made more detailed and more penetrating interviews of Yao Ming than I, and many of the older generation began to pay attention to Yao Ming when he was still in swaddling clothes; so this book is only one among many. More than anything it is a success story of someone who is deserving of all the honors he has received. Many fans of Chinese basketball who are proud of Yao Ming are looking forward to the appearance of more works about him as his remarkable career continues.

Appendix 1:   Yao Ming's Vital Statistics

Date of birth	September 12, 1980
Blood type	A
Arm length	7'2"
Native of	Shanghai
Astrological sign	Virgo
Shoe size	18 (U.S.)
Family	Basketball family
Height	7'4"
Speed in the 100-yard dash	About 15 seconds
Chinese horological animal	Monkey
Weight	295 lbs
Palm	8.2"
Favorite color	Blue
Favorite animal	Doberman dog
Favorite foods	Pork sausage, tomatoes
Favorite dishes	His mother's
Favorite holiday	National day
Favorite author	Ye Yonglie, Lao She
Favorite singer	All kinds
Favorite song	Pop
Favorite clothes	Sports, casual
Favorite city	Shanghai
Favorite country	China
Favorite movie star	Denzel Washington
Favorite movie	*La Grande Vadrouille*
Most annoyed by	Lavish praise
Most afraid of	Loneliness
Likes most to	Play high-level, exciting games

Greatest annoyance	Can't live the life of an ordinary person
Person most respected	Zhou Enlai, Liu Bei
Place to relax	Starbucks
Hobbies	Playing computer games, surfing the web, music, reading
Idols	Barkley, Sabonis, Olajuwon
Motto	Believe in yourself, youth should not be ordinary
Nicknames	Canopy over Shanghai, little giant, little giant covering the sky, the great indomitable, 'top-pick' boy, hidden dragon, Ming Dynasty

Appendix 2:   Chronology of Events

September 12, 1980	Born at Shanghai Sixth People's Hospital
1984	Age 4, kindergarten, height 3'9"
September 1986	Age 6, entered Gao An Road First Elementary School, height 4'9" primary teacher Gong Ling Zhen
September 1989	Age 9, entered Xu Jia Hui District Youth Sports School height 5'5" first coach Li Zhang Min
July 1993	Age 13, height 6'3", attended Shanghai sports basketball summer training class

1994	Age 14, height 6'5", joined Shanghai youth team, coach Li Qiu Ping
1995	Age 15, height 6'9", coach Lu Zhi Qiang
1996	Age 16, height 7'1", became a regular player on the Shanghai men's basketball team
January 1997	Age 16, height 7'2", joined Shanghai basketball team, head coach Li Qiu Ping
March 1997	Age 16, height 7' 2.2"
June 1997	Age 16, height 7' 2.8", went to Paris, France, to attend European basketball training camp
October 13, 1997	Age 17, first participated in adult game, competed in Eighth National Games, first game against Shandong
November 23, 1997	Age 17, first CBA competition, first game against Air Force Mighty Eagles
March 1998	Age 17, Shanghai Sharks take 5th place in 1997-1998 CBA season, Yao Ming wins "sports ethics award" and comes in 2nd in blocking (45 blocks), selected to CBA all-star game lineup
April 10, 1998	Age 17, selected for new national men's basketball group training team, prepares for Bangkok Asian Olympics, head coach Wang Fei
June 14, 1998	Age 17, goes to America to attend Nike youthbasketball summer camp, later praised by American reporter as "eighth wonder of the world"
September 1, 1998	Age 17, last height measurement in China, height 7'3"

November 6, 1998	Age 18, misses being chosen to Chinese men's basketball Bangkok Asian Olympics roster
December 4, 1998	Age 18, deemed "best young Asian player" by Asian Basketball League
February 3, 1999	Age 18, returns after recovery from injury, having been out of the lineup in 10 games of 1998-1999 CBA season due to bone fracture
April 1999	Age 18, Shanghai team takes 6th place in that CBA season, Yao Ming chosen "most improved player" and takes 2nd place in blocking
May 1, 1999	Age 18, signs three-year agreement with Evergreen Sports Management Corporation; five days later, Yao Ming's parents announce that the agreement is discontinued
May 8, 1999	Age 18, participates in that season's all-star game as a starter, Shanghai Sharks Assistant General Manager Li Yao Min confirms the news that Yao Ming will not take part in 1999 NBA draft
May 19, 1999	Age 18, chosen to National Men's Basketball group training team, prepares for 20th Asian Men's Basketball Championship and qualifying matches for Sydney 2000 Olympics, head coach Jiang Xingquan
August 9, 1999	Age 18, participates in Asian Men's Basketball Championship held in Japan, works together with entire team to regain Asian Men's Basketball Championship throne

February 2000	Age 19, selected to 1999 Asian All-Star team
March 2000	Age 19, Shanghai Sharks ranked 2nd for season in CBA, selected to that season's national men's basketball Class-A league all-star lineup, wins national men's basketball Class-A league rebounding, dunking and blocking titles for that season
March 2000	Age 19, chosen to national men's basketball group training team, preparing for 2000 Sydney Olympics, head coach Jiang Xingquan
September 12, 2000	Age 20, becomes regular Olympic player
September 17, 2000	Age 20, first competition against American "fourth Dream Team", scores 5 points, grabs 3 rebounds, blocks NBA "dunk king" Carter; Chinese men's basketball team takes 10th place in Sydney Olympics
November 2000	Age 20, called by ESPN new sports star with the most development potential worldwide, appears on cover of December issue of ESPN sports magazine
March 2001	Age 20, Shanghai Sharks take 2nd place for that season in the CBA, Yao Ming pockets five awards: "rebound king," "block king," "dunk king," "regular season MVP," and "year-end MVP"
May 21, 2001	Age 20, Shanghai Sharks formally announce that Yao Ming will not take part in the NBA draft that year, but indicates that he might very well go the next year

May 23, 2001	Age 20, takes part in East Asian Games, takes championship
July 29, 2001	Age 20, participates in 21st Asian Men's Basketball Championship, retains championship, individually wins three major awards: MVP, best rebounder, chosen to best lineup
August 31, 2001	Age 20, takes part in 21st World Collegiate Sports Meet held in Beijing, taking 2nd place; in semi-final match against U.S. team, Yao Ming jumped up at the last moment to block opponent's shot, assisting the Chinese team to make it into the finals 83 to 82 and ending the history of Chinese men's basketball never defeating the U.S. team in a comprehensive international sports meet
April 19, 2002	Age 21, leads Shanghai Sharks to defeat the BaYi Rockets, six-time consecutive champions and win its first CBA championship; this was the first basketball championship won by the Shanghai team in national major competition. That evening, the Shanghai Sharks formally announce that it will permit Yao Ming to take part in this year's NBA draft. At the same time, Yao Ming is selected to that season's league all-star team and chosen as the league's block king; wins "sports ethics award"
April 29, 2002	Age 21, goes to America to take part in special trial workout arranged by NBA,

	taking the first step toward joining the NBA. In America five days, Yao Ming first undergoes a rookie personal physical exam arranged by the NBA and puts on a "personal show" in front of officials and scouts from 26 teams, causing an NBA "earthquake"
May 19, 2002	Age 21, announcement of 2002 NBA draft pick order determined by lottery, Houston Rockets get the right to pick first
May 24, 2002	Age 21, Mayor Brown of Houston, in China for economic trade event, makes special trip to visit Xin Lan Cheng, secretary-general of the Chinese Basketball Association, talks up the idea of Rockets picking Yao Ming
June 9, 2002	Age 21, Houston Rockets delegation consisting of General Manager Dawson, Head Coach Tomjanovich, News Official Lewis and team Principal Goldberg arrive in China for talks with Shanghai Sharks and Chinese Basketball Association matters related to Yao Ming's going to America to play
June 21, 2002	Age 21, Chinese Basketball Association holds press briefing to announce that Yao Ming, involved with national team group practice, will not go to U.S. to attend NBA draft convention, simultaneously indicates this will have no bearing on his playing in the NBA
June 22, 2002	Age 21, Yao Ming's family holds press

	release meeting in Shanghai to announce the reaching of an agreement in principle with the Shanghai Sharks regarding the question of compensation for Yao Ming's going to play in the NBA and indicating that the matter of Yao Ming's going to America still requires the final agreement of the Chinese Basketball Association
June 26, 2002	Age 21, Chinese Basketball Association sends letter of confirmation to Rockets; Rockets convene press release meeting in Houston to announce more than 8 hours ahead of time that they will use their first pick in the draft to select Yao Ming
June 27, 2000	Age 21, picked as top rookie by Houston Rockets in 2002 NBA draft
July 25, 2002	Age 21, Houston Rockets representative arrives in Shanghai to begin talks with Shanghai Sharks relating to Yao Ming's joining the Rockets, but the two parties do not conclude any agreement
July 26, 2002	Age 21, Houston Rockets representative Goldberg and Shanghai Sharks sign written agreement regarding Yao Ming's trade
September 9, 2002	Age 21, Chinese men's basketball team takes 12th place in 14th World Men's Basketball Championship, Yao Ming selected to the best lineup of that championship
October 15, 2002	Age 22, working together with teammates, win 2nd place in Pusan Asian Games

October 20, 2002	Age 22, takes flight CA929 to America
October 28, 2002	Age 22, chosen as one of "ten best athletes nationwide" by sports department of New China News Agency
October 31, 2002	Age 22, plays in first NBA game against the Pacers, gets 0 points, later gradually improves to become Houston Rockets' core player
January 5, 2003	Age 22, jersey No. 15 is retired at the Shanghai Hu Wan Gymnasium, becoming first Chinese athlete to have jersey retired
February 10, 2003	Age 22, as a rookie, becomes the starting core center of the 52nd NBA all-star game; public opinion says Jordan will pass the baton to the hands of younger players like Yao Ming
April 20, 2003	Returns to China after first season in the NBA.
May 11, 2003	Leads fundraising telethon for SARS relief.
October 1, 2003	With the Chinese national team, defeats defending champions South Korea to clinch Asian basketball championship and assure China's berth in 2004 Olympic basketball competition.

Appendix 3. Yao Ming's NBA Skills Statistics and Competition Record (as of February 20, 2003)

Statistic Item	Statistic Number	Rookie Ranking	League Ranking
Times appearing on court	52	-	-
Times starting	42	-	-
Average time	27.7	6	-
Points per game	13.0	3	-
Scoring percentage	52.9%	2	4
Free-throw percentage	77.4%	5	-
Rebounds per game	8.10	2	21
Offensive rebounds	2.40	3	30
Defensive rebounds	5.70	2	25
Blocks per game	1.98	1	14
Assists per game	1.6	11	-
Interceptions pergame	0.31	-	-
Double doubles	16	2	20
Effectiveness coefficient	17.75	1	37
Turnovers per game	1.96	-	-
Fouls per game	2.80	-	-

Appendix 4: Yao Ming's Game Report: Season 1

Date	Game Report	Points Scored
2.22	85-100 Mavericks	18

2.20	107-89 Suns	12
2.19	99-106 Lakers	24
2.15	94-82 Heat	10
2.13	106-76 Jazz	15
2.12	101-103 Jazz	25
2.6	102-105 Cavaliers	14
2.5	89-103 Timberwolves	12
2.3	105-89 Kings	18
2.1	121-101 Timberwolves	24
1.30	81-104 Mavericks	20
1.28	100-95 Grizzlies	13
1.27	98-100 Bulls	14
1.25	74-98 Pistons	6
1.22	86-107 Mavericks	6
1.21	82-87 Spurs	11
1.18	108-104 Lakers	10
1.16	102-96 Suns	11
1.14	101-92 Celtics	10
1.12	87-85 Nuggets	6
1.11	75-84 Hawks	9
1.9	91-81 Magic	23
1.8	94-86 Timberwolves	9
1.5	84-86 Warriors	11
2003.1.1	103-80 Bucks	16
12.30	97-85 Hornets	12
12.28	83-99 Knicks	17
12.24	91-96 Jazz	18
12.22	86-98 Timberwolves	12
12.21	101-82 Hawks	17
12.19	95-83 Pacers	29

12.17	105-100 Heat	15
12.15	83-94 Clippers	16
12.14	109-114 Grizzlies	18
12.11	103-96 Kings	17
12.08	97-72 76ers	18
12.07	96-98 Hornets	16
12.04	89-75 Spurs	27
12.02	84-103 Kings	8
11.30	83-72 Supersonics	6
11.28	91-84 Warriors	14
11.27	71-77 Trailblazers	10
11.25	89-90 Clippers	4
11.23	93-86 Wizards	18
11.22	90-103 Mavericks	30
11.20	97-80 Cavaliers	9
11.18	93-89 Lakers	20
11.16	87-88 Suns	10
11.13	86-83 Trailblazers	7
11.10	111-104 Warriors	3
11.06	97-104 Supersonics	0
11.03	88-76 Raptors	8
11.02	83-74 Nuggets	2
2002.10.31	82-91 Pacers	0

About the Author

Chunfei Xiao was born in 1972 in Hunan Province. In 1994 he graduated from the Chinese Department of Central China Technical University, and he has worked as a reporter for the China Sports News Agency and the Guangxi branch of the Xinhua (New China) News Agency. He is currently a reporter for the Shanghai branch of the Xinhua News Agency.

About the Translator

Philip Robyn has translated and edited many Chinese books, including scientific and technical writings in such diverse fields as geology, astronomy, medicine, and engineering. He has translated the text of the exhibits (from English to Chinese) at the Hong Kong Space Museum, as well as such literary pieces as Liu Binyan's well-known reportorial exposé "At the Bridge Site" (Zai Qiao Liang Gong Di Shang). Mr. Robyn is a senior computer programmer at the University of California, Berkeley. He has traveled extensively in China and is an avid student of Chinese internal martial arts.